Uncertainty in Information Systems:
An Introduction to Techniques and Applications

ADVANCED TOPICS IN COMPUTER SCIENCE SERIES

Consulting Editors

Professor V. J. RAYWARD SMITH
School of Information Systems
University of East Anglia
Norwich, UK

This series of texts is aimed at postgraduates and advanced students of computer science in colleges and universities. The titles will also be invaluable reading for researchers in this field.

ADVANCED TOPICS IN COMPUTER SCIENCE

Uncertainty in Information Systems:
An Introduction to Techniques and Applications

Anthony Hunter
Department of Computing
Imperial College of Science, Technology and Medicine

The McGraw-Hill Companies

London · New York · St Louis · San Francisco · Auckland · Bogotá ·
Caracas ·Lisbon · Madrid · Milan · Montreal · New Delhi · Panama · Paris ·
San Juan · São Paulo · Singapore · Sydney · Tokyo · Toronto

Published by
McGraw-Hill Publishing Company
Shoppenhangers Road, Maidenhead, Berkshire, SL6 2QL, England
Telephone 01682 23432
Facsimile 01628 770224

British Library Cataloguing in Publication Data
The CIP data of this title is available from the British Library, UK

Library of Congress Cataloging-in-Publication Data
The CIP data of this title is available from the Library of Congress,
Washington DC, USA

McGraw-Hill

A Division of The McGraw-Hill Companies

1234 BL 99876

Typeset by Anthony Hunter and printed and bound in Great Britain by
Biddles Ltd, Guildford, Surrey.

Printed on permanent paper in compliance with ISO Standard 9706

Contents

Preface

Aim of the book

This book is intended to highlight the significance of uncertainty in the management of information, introduce methods of modelling uncertain information, and discuss current and potential applications of such methods in information systems. Towards this end, the text will provide the reader with the following:

- A discussion of the kinds of information that are problematical.

- A discussion of the ways this impinges upon systems — for example,

    - null values in relational databases
    - heuristics in rule-based decision-support systems
    - vagueness of keywords used in information retrieval
    - appropriateness of cases in case-based decision-support systems
    - conflicts in requirements specifications.

- An exposition of means for modelling uncertain information — including probability theory, possibility theory, fuzzy set theory and non-classical logics.

- A review of the current and potential applications of handling uncertainty in information systems.

The emphasis of the book will be on providing a "feel" for the problems and possible solutions for handling uncertainty in information systems rather than on providing a very comprehensive and technical coverage of the area.

Overview of the book

The book is split into the following three parts:

Part 1: Introduction and background

The first two chapters will introduce problems, importance, and possibilities of handling uncertainty in information systems. Chapter 1 focuses on the diversity of uncertainty in information. Chapter 2 focuses on the need to adopt formal approaches to uncertainty. It includes an introduction to classical logic and set theory.

Part 2: Techniques for uncertainty

The next four chapters (Chapters 3 – 6) are an exposition of means for modelling uncertain information. These will focus on probabilistic information, fuzzy information, default information, and inconsistent information, respectively. This coverage will provide us with a range of techniques for handling uncertainty in information.

Part 3: Applications in information systems

The following four chapters (Chapters 7 – 10) review the current and potential applications of handling uncertainty in information systems. These will focus on knowledge-based systems, database systems, online information systems, and systems engineering, respectively. In each of these chapters, we will draw upon techniques presented in Part 2. The final chapter (Chapter 11) will discuss the outlook for uncertainty in information systems.

Intended readership

Since uncertainty in information systems is such a widespread and increasingly important issue, increasing numbers of users of information technology are interested in addressing the topic. Furthermore, there is a wide range of applications where uncertainty handling techniques could be useful. With this in mind, it is intended that the book will be of interest to many people in IT, including postgraduates, researchers, developers, and managers of advanced information systems, and those interested in information strategies in organizations. It could also be used as supplementary reading for undergraduate courses that cover aspects of information systems.

Anticipated pre-requisites for readers

There are now many formalisms in IT, such as relational algebra, relational calculus, dataflow diagrams, entity-relationship diagrams, inheritance hierarchies, conceptual modelling, and Z, and for many users, such formalisms bring significant advantages. This trend for formalisms is reflected in this book. It is hoped that readers who appreciate that, in general, there is value in such methods, will be happy with the approach of this book. Although, it is our aim that this text should also be easily accessible.

It is intended that there will be no pre-requisites. However, the following will be helpful: (1) Some exposure to logic and probability theory, though introductory material is included; (2) Some appreciation of the limitations of mainstream IT to handle uncertain information, though this is discussed in the book; and (3) Some awareness of information systems such as relational databases, knowledge-based systems, work-group systems, and information retrieval systems.

Acknowledgements

This book has greatly benefitted from contributions and feedback from Philippe Besnard, James Cussens, Dov Gabbay, Pablo Gervas, Jerome Lang, Kevin Lano, Bashar Nuseibeh, Sanjay Modgil, Simon Parsons, Philippe Smets and Nic Wilson.

The research was partially funded by the UK EPSRC as part of the VOILA project (GR J15483) and the CEC as part of ESPRIT DRUMS II project.

Anthony Hunter
Department of Computing
Imperial College of Science, Technology and Medicine
180 Queen's Gate
London SW7 2BZ
UK

Email: abh@doc.ic.ac.uk

Chapter 1

Uncertainty in Information

1.1 Introduction

It would be impossible for an organization to survive if it only made decisions
with information that was certain. Constantly, members of an organization
have to handle a wide variety of kinds of uncertain information in order to
fulfil their role in the organization. Consider the following examples.

- In a financial trading company, much information on economic, corporate, and market indicators is analysed to predict future performance of investments.

- In a market research agency, much statistical and textual information is collated and analysed for identifying market behaviour.

- In an engineering design consultancy, empirical, theoretical, and heuristic information is exploited in order to design products that meet client specifications.

- In a magazine editorial office, much textual information is collated and used in writing new articles. The quantity and diversity of this information calls for heuristics to handle it.

- In an insurance claims department, textual information from claimants, witnesses, assessors, and advisors, is used to determine whether a claim should be accepted or rejected.

1

- In a law firm, much textual information in the form of legislation, contracts, and other legal documentation, is analysed, in conjunction with legal principles and heuristics, to provide advice.

In these applications the diverse kinds of information might involve probabilistic, fuzzy, default, and inconsistent information. For the users of textual information, such as in an editorial office, insurance claims department, or legal firm, there are many kinds of uncertainty in interpreting textual information. Similarly, for the users of statistical information such as in market research and engineering design there are many problems handling and interpreting numerical information. Furthermore, for all the organizations in these examples, merging different kinds of information, often from many different sources, with differing reliabilities, is fraught with uncertainties.

In each of these examples, the users of the information are attempting to model some aspect of the real-world. They can then analyse these models for the purposes of their work. The ability to model and reason with uncertain information is therefore essential for the people undertaking these kinds of tasks.

The nature of uncertainty in information is complex. Many factors affect the types of uncertainty, sources of uncertainty and the degrees of uncertainty [Mot95]. Nevertheless, there are many strategies that users adopt for aggregating such factors in order to minimize the potential negative ramifications of operating under uncertainty. Indeed, via learning, humans, and more generally, organizations, can become highly adept at using uncertain information.

The ubiquitous usage of uncertain information by organizations contrasts sharply with the low level of computer-based handling of uncertain information. Whilst many theoretical models have been proposed for the management of uncertainty, present generation information systems have very limited capabilities in this regard.

The situation is set to change as the expanding role of information technology means that handling of uncertain information will become increasingly significiant. Indeed as uncertainty pervades virtually any real-world scenario, uncertainty handling must be incorporated into any information system that attempts to provide a substantive model of the real-world. Even now diverse types of information system such as database systems, information retrieval systems, expert systems, and office automation systems are currently being developed to incorporate and use formal models for uncertain information.

The development of information systems to handle uncertainty is not technology driven. Increasingly, there are demands for people to handle more complex information, more quickly, more reliably, and in particular in a more natural and intuitive fashion. Only by developing and incorporating appropriate models of uncertain information in information systems can these demands be met.

In the following we discuss these types of uncertainty, and explain how they can be handled in particular types of advanced information system.

1.2 Concepts for uncertainty

Whilst we will provide an informal classification of uncertainty, it is clear that there is actually no universally accepted classification. This is perhaps not surprising given that classifications for uncertain information are inextricably linked with fields such as linguistics and cognition. Take, for example, terms such as uncertainty, imprecision, ignorance, vagueness, and ambiguity. Other researchers have attempted the same goal, including [KC93, Sme95], though with different results to ours. The following attempt is intended to indicate possibilities rather than be definitive.

First we assume information is composible. So from some items of information, we can generate other items of information. For example, a database record for a member of staff is composed from information about name, address, qualifications, role and salary.

Second we assume that some information can be described as correct according to some measure and that some can be described as incorrect. For example, for a database record for a member of staff, we can ask them whether their name and address is entered correctly.

Third we assume we can have expectations about information, such as the presence of certain information. For example, for a database on staff, we expect information on name, address, and salary for each member of staff. Note the expectation is that this information exists, rather than that we know what the actual information is. So for the staff member "John Smith" we expect there to be an entry for his salary, though we don't necessarily have an expectation about the actual salary.

Using these assumptions, we can classify information as in Table 1.1. Below are fuller definitions of these classes.

Accurate Information is accurate when all expected information is present and correct, and it is error-free.

3

	All expected information is present	Some expected information is absent
All incorrect information is absent	Accurate	Incomplete
Some incorrect information is present	Incompatible	Approximate

Table 1.1: Classification of information according to the presence or absence of expected information and the presence or absence of incorrect information

Incomplete Information is incomplete when all the information present is correct but some expected information is absent. This could occur because the information is open to multiple interpretation, underspecified, vague, or just deficient. As an example, consider the ambiguous statement "this food is hot", which could be interpreted as "this food is spicy" or "this food is very warm". So if we are expected to ascertain from this statement which of these two interpretations hold, this ambiguity means the information is incomplete. As another example consider the staff database again. Suppose there is no salary for a particular member of staff. This missing data means the information is incomplete.

Incompatible Information is incompatible when there is a conflict between correct and incorrect information present. For example, suppose in the staff records, we have an employee who has a date of promotion a year after a date of retirement. This staff record is incompatible since there is an inconsistency with our common-sense knowledge about people not being promoted after retirement.

Approximate Information is approximate when some expected information is missing and possibly there are conflicts between the correct and incorrect information. For example, we could believe that it is likely that it will rain soon because there are dark clouds in the sky. However, this belief is not totally accurate becuse this reasoning relies on a general rule that does not take account of all relevant information. In other words, the information is incomplete. Furthermore, the inference of rain made from the general rule could be incompatible with other information that we have such as the barometric pressure is rising sharply.

There are interesting informal relationships between different kinds of uncertainty, such as the information maximality principle [Sme95], where the more focussed some information is, the more likely it is that it will be incorrect. For example, if we predict the outcome of a football game by proposing the winner, we are more likely to be correct than if we propose the winner together with the score of the game. Another way of viewing this principle is that there is a pay-off between completeness and correctness.

Using the above classification, we can delineate meanings for certainty and uncertainty.

Certainty We believe or use information with certainty when it is accurate. In other words, certain information is a synonym for accurate information

Uncertainty Uncertainty exists in information when it is incomplete, incorrect, or approximate.

We use any of the synonyms inaccurate, inexact, and imprecise, for information that is significantly uncertain. We sometimes use the synonym erroneous information for incorrect information. In the Glossary, we consider some further important adjectives for describing uncertain information.

Clearly it is difficult to define words for uncertainty so that they are appropriate for all users or all contexts. However, when certain formal assumptions are adopted – for example, the axioms of probability, or axioms of some logic – then some classifications can become much more meaningful and useful. We aim to show this in the following chapters.

1.3 Types of uncertain information

Uncertainty in information is not a homogeneous concept. Rather there are clearly diverse types that require distinct means for handling. Here we consider probabilistic, fuzzy, inconsistent, and default forms of information.

Probabilistic information Most people have recourse to using probabilistic information at some time — take betting for instance. Indeed, people can reason very effectively with complex tasks of assessing probabilities and predicting values by various strategies [TK74].

Probabilistic information is widespread. Many organizations keep large databases of information. Some extract useful probabilistic relationships from such information. Take for example credit scoring agencies who analyse large numbers of past cases to find significant correlations between customer details and defaults such as customers with certain postcodes, or customers in certain age-groups, are more likely to default on repayments.

But people don't always need large amounts of data to generate probabilities. Often beliefs and heuristics are presented in the form of probabilities. For example, in horse racing, the odds are generated from an aggregation of predominantly subjective factors.

Fuzzy information Most concepts used in human reasoning are to some extent vague or fuzzy. Investing in a company with a "high growth rate" seems more interesting than investing in one with a "low growth rate". Many fuzzy concepts can be useful because, depending on the context, they can be delineated.

For example, a small-to-medium enterprise (SME) is a company that has a turnover of say less than $500,000 per annum. Suppose we hear an economic forecast that states that SMEs will benefit disproportionately well in the coming upturn in the economy. Also suppose we consider two very similar companies A and B, where A has a turnover of $510,000, and B has a turnover of $5,000,000. Neither A nor B are strictly SMEs. But, since it is reasonable to regard the boundary as fuzzy, A can be considered an SME, whereas B cannot really. Now, a rational inference from all this would be that A will outperform B, all other factors being equal.

Inconsistent information There are many situations in which some information and its contrary appear. In some situations it is useful, such as in a tax collection database, since it can initiate profitable enquiries. In other situations it is undesirable, such as in a bank database on customer accounts, where the inconsistency needs to be located and the database revised.

Maintaining absolute consistency is not always possible since it is not always possible to resolve it. Often it is not even desirable since this can lead to the loss of important information. Rather than resolving conflicts immediately it can be better to support different views for the interim. This involves the ability to represent the information, to reason rationally with the information, to diagnose the likely cause of the inconsistency, and to propose necessary actions in response.

For example, in capturing the requirements of a number of users for a new computer network, each user is influenced by their knowledge, responsibilities, and commitments. Inevitably, the different perspectives of those involved in the process interact, giving rise to the possibility of conflict between perspectives, and to a need for co-ordination.

As another example, consider the problem of merging two sales department databases. Suppose, both databases have a record for the same customer, and suppose that some of the data in these two records is mutually contradictory. Information is not rejected arbitrarily. Rather strategies are used to support the contradictory information until an informed selection can be made.

Default information Loosely, default information is information that is used in the absence of opposition or in the absence of a better alternative. The notion of defaults covers a seemingly diverse variety of information including heuristics, hypotheses, conjectures, null values in data, closed world assumptions for databases, and some qualitative abstractions of probabilistic information.

Defaults are a natural and very common form of information. Whilst they do not always give the right answer, they are generally useful. Indeed, it is inconceivable that we could lead our lives without constant recourse to defaults. Consider a normal working day. If you commute, you don't check that the trains or buses are operating before you leave the house, you assume they are until you learn otherwise. When you get to work, you assume your office is in the same place, unless told otherwise; you assume that your responsibilities are unchanged, unless instructed otherwise, and so on.

Inconsistent information is a form of incompatible information. Probabilistic, fuzzy and default information are forms of approximate information. We use these forms of approximate information when we lack certain information. In general, approximate information can be obtained from subjective evaluations or derived from past experience, and as such it is an estimate that can conflict with the behaviour of the thing it models.

7

1.4 Levels of uncertainty

Uncertain information can be used in many different roles. To develop appropriate strategies, it is useful to adopt the terms "object-level" information and "meta-level" information, defined as follows.

Object-level information Within an organization, the purpose of an information system is to handle information for some benefit to the organization. Object-level information is that which an end-user is using. The user is aware of the existence of object-level information in the system. Queries to, and answers from, the system are in terms of the object-level information.

Meta-level information In order for an information system to handle object-level information, there is a need for extra information about the object-level information, and about the possible users of that information. This extra information is meta-level information. Whilst meta-level information is used to facilitate the information system meeting the end-user's needs, it is not actually seen, or used directly, by the end-user. For instance meta-level information can be used to increase or decrease the amount of information given in answer to a query, whereas the answer is actually object-level information.

To illustrate this, we consider the increasingly important technologies of decision-support systems, information retrieval systems, and softbots.

1.4.1 Information retrieval systems

In information retrieval systems, object-level information is often stored in "documents". For example, in a database for company analyses, these could be articles written in the financial press, market research reports, or trade association reports. The information in the documents might be uncertain: It might involve defaults such as "sales of trucks in the UK are significantly affected by the growth in the economy", or it might involve statistical information, such as a breakdown of consumer preferences in purchasing cars. In contrast, the meta-level information includes information that could assist the user in finding a document of interest within the information repository.

In information retrieval, a common form of interaction is for the user to offer a set of keywords. These are then used by the information retrieval system to identify a set of documents. The aim is for the probability that a set of documents meets the user needs is high.

In current information retrieval technology, there is an emphasis on using probabilistic information at the meta-level for relating keywords with documents. However, using other kinds of information such as fuzzy and default will become essential. This will be particularly important to analyse the meaning of the queries — for example by using more sophisticated parsing, lexicons, and thesauri, for keywords — and to determine the intentions of the user with respect to the query.

Currently most information retrieval systems are used for either enhancing relational databases or for text retrieval. In both these cases much of the problem of uncertain information is with meta-level information.

1.4.2 Decision-support systems

Decision-support tools are already used profitably in organization tasks including credit-scoring, financial trading, and administration. Two main approaches to decision-support systems are rule-based systems and case-based systems.

Rule-based systems use "rules" to represent information ranging from definitions and regulations to heuristics and rules of conjecture. In these, uncertain information is predominantly object-level.

Case-based systems use "cases" to represent information: For example, a decision-support system for advising on insolvency might have instances of insolvency as cases. For this approach to decision-support, the user is usually interested in locating cases of interest. This is done by delineating the type of case that is of interest, often by keywords. In this sense, case-based reasoning has similarities with information retrieval, and as such, there may be uncertain information at both the object-level and the meta-level.

Unfortunately, few of the current decision-support systems use formal approaches to handling uncertainty. This puts these applications at a potential disadvantage. However, a formal approach that is gaining acceptance is that of causal probabilistic networks, also known as Bayesian networks. This offers a graphical representation of conditional probabilities and can be handled by computationally viable algorithms for inferencing. This approach provides a lucid, yet formal, means for representing and reasoning with some kinds of uncertain information.

1.4.3 Softbots

Interest in softbots has increased as a result of the rapidly widening horizons for information highways, or infobahns. Collectively, softbots are "intelligent software agents" that are instructed to seek, filter, and generally manage, information for a user. Hence, they are of interest in a wide variety of roles, such as filtering incoming emails, bridging heterogeneous legacy databases, consistency checking in databases, filtering newswire information, navigating online libraries, and so on.

Most softbots use uncertain information at the meta-level to capture the user's information interests and needs. In addition, some softbots handle uncertain information at the object-level. For example, in handling inconsistencies resulting from consistency checking, or handling null values when merging datasets,

Unsurprisingly, much work in softbots has been by using *ad hoc* techniques. However, as with all applications discussed here, it is clear that there will be increasing pressure to adopt formal approaches to uncertain information.

1.5 Imperatives for using uncertain information

The roles of information systems are clearly diverse. Hence, addressing the problem of uncertainty in information systems is a broad subject. Nevertheless, there are also a number of common themes in addressing uncertainty in information. Perhaps the strongest theme is that dealing with uncertainty is a complex and difficult task, requiring a range of formal techniques [Fox86, Saf87, Cla90, Par96].

Modelling uncertainty involves a significant dilemma [Mot95]. In order to minimize the mistakes from using uncertain information, there is a need to adopt a rich and powerful model. However, information systems usually need simple and efficient representation and reasoning facilities.

Often the purpose of information systems is to support "good" decision-making. We can see that there is a general problem of dealing with the trade-offs between risk-avoidance and economies in the process of decision making. Ideally our information system should be able to assess in a given context, how accurate the information should be. Essentially the system makes some utility-theoretic assessment. So if the problem is significant in some sense, our information system may take care to collect as much relevant information as possible from the environment, and to reason extensively with this. Whereas if the problem is less significant, less information would be collected, and it would be analysed far less thoroughly. In general an optimal compromise should be realizable.

Updating is another key aspect to the trade-offs between risk-avoidance and economies in our information system. Updating can be expensive, both in storage and time. Furthermore, it can be difficult to decide how to update, for information can be conflicting, and there may be no obvious resolution.

It therefore seems that for our information system to succeed in the real-world, the formalisms on which it is based need to be both sophisticated and efficient. Furthermore, if we are to be confident that our agent is to succeed, then we need to be rigorous in our developments, and we need to demonstrate that certain properties of our agent hold. We expand this argument in the next chapter.

Chapter 2

Formal Approaches to Uncertainty

2.1 Introduction

In order to handle uncertain information, we first need sufficiently expressive means to represent it. Then we need to incorporate a reasoning component into our information systems in order to derive answers from the uncertain information. Also, as discussed in the previous chapter, we assume that given the diverse kinds of uncertainty in information, we will need to develop a range of techniques.

2.2 Formalization of uncertainty

Adopting *ad hoc* approaches to computer-based handling of uncertain information can easily become counter-productive. Using computers in an organization is in some respects like delegating. Tasks are delegated when the delegator has confidence about the nature of outcome from the delegate. So for example, there is confidence in delegating payroll activities to computers because of the well-understood principles of arithmetic and accountancy. With handling uncertain information, the behaviour of even small datasets can be difficult to predict. Therefore, if we are to delegate handling of uncertain information, we should only do so within the context of well-understood principles.

2.2.1 The need for a high-level language

First, let us consider some general requirements for handling uncertainty in information systems. There are many constraints on an information system, some internally imposed, and some externally imposed. Internally, it has only limited information storage capabilities and it is also limited in its ability to process complex information quickly. Externally, it is limited by the information that the environment gives it: information will usually be incomplete, and also approximate in one or more ways. Finally there may be changes in the information over time, either by internal or external updates. These various constraints mean that our information system is forced to adopt appropriate forms of reasoning.

In addition to these general constraints, we focus in this book on applications where there is a need for the representation of information in a readily accessible and lucid form for the engineer or end-user. This need is prevalent in a wide range of systems including relational databases, decision-support systems, information retrieval systems, information filtering systems, and requirements engineering tools.

For example, decision-support tools when used by human decision-makers can enhance the decision-makers' performance. However, if the decision-support tool is opaque — i.e. the tool does not explain or justify its reasoning — then the confidence that the user has in the tool's output is decreased. Moreover, if the tool is opaque, then the user cannot qualify or adapt the output in the context of the wider sphere of information and experience that the user has access to.

We therefore assume that we need a range of formal systems for handling uncertainty, and that each of these will incorporate a high-level language for representing uncertain information.

Neural networks are also aimed at handling uncertain information. They are predominantly "black boxes", trained to relate inputs to outputs, but not able to provide explanations or justifications for outputs. A number of financial organizations in the UK and the US are utilizing neural networks, where they are proving to be increasingly reliable, and useful tools in highly delineated domains. For example, consider a neural network trained to handle the decision to buy, or sell, US dollars for Deutschmarks, by using indicators including unemployment rates, inflation rates, balance of trade, and government deficit. Unfortunately, if the "black box" identifies some complex combination of inputs causing the decision to buy, the user has no understanding of how, or why that decision was reached.

2.2.2 Concepts for formalization

We now consider how we approach uncertainty in information and clarify some of the terms that we are using.

Modelling The process of developing a formal model of some system. The model should emulate the behaviour of the system in some sense. The formal model is presented using some formal language. A model is then a set of formal statements in the language. Since the model is information, if there is some uncertainty in the model, then the model will constitute uncertain information.

Reasoning When using a formal language, we assume the statements in the language will be reasoned with in some particular way. This is some method that supports query answering, and optionally deriving inferences. In this book we present reasoning by using some set of axioms or (proof) rules that define the allowed operations.

Formalism A formal language for modelling together with some definition for reasoning with sets of statements in the language. We also use the terms formalism, formal system, and formal method, synonymously.

Handling In order to use uncertain information in information systems, we need to use handling techniques. This includes technology for mechanizing the model, and so support automated reasoning. It also includes tool support for engineers and users to develop and analyse the model.

As an example, consider a relational language that is used in relational databases as a formal language. A set of relations is then a model. In a payroll system, the relations might capture data about employee names, address, and salaries, together with data about bank accounts, pay day, and tax schedules. Relational algebra, or relational calculus, is then the means for reasoning with a relational database. A database management system then provides the means for handling the information.

As another example, consider a simple expert system. Here the language could be production rules, which are of the form "If ... Then" rules. In a tax advisory application, the rules could model tax regulations. Inferencing methods based on deriving the consequent of the rule, if the antecedent holds, then constitute the reasoning method. An expert system shell then provides the means for handling a set of rules.

In order to clarify some of these ideas, we consider classical formalisms in the next section. Classical formalisms have many desirable features and properties for representing and reasoning with information, but as we will see in subsequent chapters they cannot capture all kinds of uncertainty satisfactorily. Hence in later chapters we will consider other formal approaches to uncertainty, such as those based on probability theory, fuzzy set theory, and non-classical logic. Though most of these other approaches are actually derived from classical formalisms.

2.3 Classical formalisms

The value of classical logic and classical set theory is in their precise languages and manipulation rules. Whilst its utility is restricted in reasoning with inconsistent and approximate information, we will consider adaptations, in later chapters, that handle a wider range of uncertainty. In the following subsections, we review classical logics and classical set theory. For more comprehensive coverage, see [Hod77] for a good accessible introduction to logic, and [Den86, Liu85] for a good introduction to classical formalisms in general.

2.3.1 Classical propositional logic

First, we need a formal language. Let us base this on a set of atomic propositions. For example,

$$paris\text{-}is\text{-}the\text{-}capital\text{-}of\text{-}france$$

$$washington\text{-}is\text{-}the\text{-}capital\text{-}of\text{-}usa$$

$$ford\text{-}makes\text{-}cars$$

$$madrid\text{-}is\text{-}the\text{-}capital\text{-}of\text{-}australia$$

We assume propositions are either *true* or *false*. Clearly, the last proposition in the list above is *false*, and the rest are *true*.

We can extend the language by using connectives including conjunction, denoted $\wedge$, disjunction, denoted $\vee$, negation, denoted $\neg$, equivalence, denoted $\leftrightarrow$, and implication, denoted $\rightarrow$. So if α and β are propositions, then $\alpha \wedge \beta$ is a proposition, $\alpha \vee \beta$ is a proposition, $\alpha \leftrightarrow \beta$ is a proposition, $\alpha \rightarrow \beta$ is a proposition, and $\neg \alpha$ is a proposition. For example, *paris-is-the-capital-of-france* ∧ *washington-is-the-capital-of-usa*

canberra-is-the-capital-of-australia ∨ *madrid-is-the-capital-of-australia*

¬*madrid-is-the-capital-of-australia*

We can extend the evaluation of truth and falsity by using truth tables. For the truth table for negation (Table 2.1), if we know the truth value for α (the left column), then we can calulate the truth value for ¬α (the right column), and vice versa.

α	¬α
true	*false*
false	*true*

Table 2.1: Truth table for negation

For the truth table for conjunction (Table 2.2), if we know the value of α and β, then we can calculate the value for their conjunction. The truth tables for disjunction (Table 2.3), implication (Table 2.4), and equivalence (Table 2.5) are used similarly. So for example the following propositions are true, assuming the truth-values given to the atomic propositions earlier.

paris-is-the-capital-of-france ∧ *washington-is-the-capital-of-usa*

canberra-is-the-capital-of-australia ∨ *madrid-is-the-capital-of-australia*

¬*madrid-is-the-capital-of-australia*

Whereas the following proposition is false.

canberra-is-the-capital-of-australia ∧ *madrid-is-the-capital-of-australia*

Since using truth tables can be inefficient, it is better to use proof rules to reason with sets of propositions. The following set of proof rules (Table 2.6) gives the same reasoning as the above truth tables in the sense that an inference follows from the data using the proof rules if and only if whenever the data is *true*, then the inference is *true*, according to the truth tables.

17

α	β	$\alpha \land \beta$
true	*true*	*true*
true	*false*	*false*
false	*true*	*false*
false	*false*	*false*

Table 2.2: Truth table for conjunction

α	β	$\alpha \lor \beta$
true	*true*	*true*
true	*false*	*true*
false	*true*	*true*
false	*false*	*false*

Table 2.3: Truth table for disjunction

α	β	$\alpha \rightarrow \beta$
true	*true*	*true*
true	*false*	*false*
false	*true*	*true*
false	*false*	*true*

Table 2.4: Truth table for implication

α	β	$\alpha \leftrightarrow \beta$
true	*true*	*true*
true	*false*	*false*
false	*true*	*false*
false	*false*	*true*

Table 2.5: Truth table for equivalence

Conjunct introduction	If we can derive α and derive β, then we can derive $\alpha \wedge \beta$.
Conjunct elimination	If we can derive $\alpha \wedge \beta$, then we can derive α and β.
Disjunct introduction	If we can derive α, then we can derive $\alpha \vee \beta$.
Disjunct elimination	If we can derive $\alpha \vee \beta$, and when we hypothetically assume α, we can derive γ, and when we hypothetically assume β, we can derive γ, then we can derive γ.
Implies introduction	If when we hypothetically assume α, we can derive β, then we can derive $\alpha \rightarrow \beta$.
Implies elimination	If we can derive α, and we can derive $\alpha \rightarrow \beta$, then we can derive β.
Negate elimination	If we can derive α and derive $\neg \alpha$, then we can derive any β.
Negate introduction	If when we assume α, we can derive some β and $\neg \beta$, then we can derive $\neg \alpha$.
Equivalence introduction	If we can derive $\alpha \rightarrow \beta$, and we can derive $\beta \rightarrow \alpha$, then we can derive $\alpha \leftrightarrow \beta$.
Equivalence elimination	If we can derive $\alpha \leftrightarrow \beta$, then we can derive $\alpha \rightarrow \beta$, and we can derive $\beta \rightarrow \alpha$,

Table 2.6: Proof rules for classical logic

We use these proof rules by assuming some set of propositions, and then try to derive further propositions from the set, using the proof rules. Each proof rule is in an "If ... then" format. In other words, if the antecedent holds, then the consequent holds. So for example, if we can derive α and we can derive β, then by conjunct introduction, we can derive $\alpha \wedge \beta$. In general, we can derive a proposition either if it is in the database, or if it has been derived by a proof rule. We can use the proof rules repeatedly to build a chain of steps to derive an inference.

For the proof rules, where we hypothetically assume a proposition, we are effectively adding the proposition temporarily to the database. Once we have verified whether the antecedent of the proof rule holds, we remove the hypothetical assumption.

For example, we could have the following database. Imagine the database has been compiled by a reader of a business article that contains an ambiguity. The reader wasn't sure which of the following hold according to the article:

$$acme\text{-}makes\text{-}software$$

$$acme\text{-}makes\text{-}hardware$$

The reader had discovered from the article that if *acme-makes-software* then *acme-increases-workforce* holds and if *acme-makes-hardware* then *acme-increases-workforce* holds. The reader represents these findings as a set of propositions as follows.

$$acme\text{-}makes\text{-}software \lor acme\text{-}makes\text{-}hardware$$

$$acme\text{-}makes\text{-}software \rightarrow acme\text{-}increases\text{-}workforce$$

$$acme\text{-}makes\text{-}hardware \rightarrow acme\text{-}increases\text{-}workforce$$

Now suppose the reader wants to know if *acme-increases-workforce*. Using the first proposition together with the the second and third propositions, the following can be derived by using disjunct elimination and implies elimination.

$$acme\text{-}increases\text{-}workforce$$

However, suppose the reader also had the following information, and from it wants to know whether *acme-good-investment* holds.

$$acme\text{-}makes\text{-}software \rightarrow acme\text{-}good\text{-}investment$$

Since the reader cannot derive *acme-makes-software*, then she cannot derive *acme-good-investment*.

To simplify our exposition in this book, we often present proof rules in a format where the data, or previously derived formulae, are written on a line, and the inference that can follow, below the line. For example, we can present implies elimination as follows.

$$\frac{\alpha \to \beta, \ \alpha}{\beta}$$

Using this form we can present further proof rules that hold for classical logic, such as *modus tollens*, as follows.

$$\frac{\alpha \to \beta, \ \neg\beta}{\neg\alpha}$$

Similarly, we can present the resolution proof rule as follows.

$$\frac{\alpha \lor \beta, \ \neg\beta \lor \gamma}{\alpha \lor \gamma}$$

Resolution also has the following two proof rules as special cases.

$$\frac{\alpha \lor \beta, \ \neg\beta}{\alpha} \quad \frac{\beta, \ \neg\beta \lor \gamma}{\gamma}$$

Yet another example is double negation elimination.

$$\frac{\neg\neg\alpha}{\alpha}$$

Modus tollens, resolution, and double negation elimination are just a few of a number of proof rules that can be shown to be valid for classical logic.

When we can prove a formula α following from Δ using the proof rules, we can represent this as $\Delta \vdash \alpha$, where $\vdash$ is called the classical consequence relation.

2.3.2 Classical predicate logic

Whilst propositional logic can be useful for a variety of applications, there is a requirement for a more general language. This includes the need to write universal rules such as the following, where X is some variable.

For all X, if X is a human, then X is male or X is female

Similarly, there is a need for existential statements such as the following.

21

There exists an X such that X is the president of the USA

Furthermore, there is a need for more complex statements such as the following.

For all X, if X is a human, there is a Y such that Y is the parent of X.

In order to make this notation a little more succinct, we present these statements using the logical connectives used above, together with predicates, and the symbols $\forall$ denoting *For all*, and $\exists$ denoting *There exists*.

$$\forall X \; human(X) \rightarrow male(X) \vee female(X)$$

$$\exists X \; president\text{-}of\text{-}the\text{-}usa(X)$$

$$\forall X \; human(X) \rightarrow \exists Y parent(Y, X)$$

We assume some domain over which variables can range. In other words, we assume some set, where elements of that set can be used to instantiate the variables. For example, we could use the domain of people in London. So this includes *john-major*, *margaret-thatcher*, etc. Hence, we have formulae such as the following.

$$human(john\text{-}major) \rightarrow male(john\text{-}major) \vee female(john\text{-}major)$$

$$human(margaret\text{-}thatcher) \rightarrow$$
$$(male(margaret\text{-}thatcher) \vee female(margaret\text{-}thatcher))$$

Once a predicate statement is instantiated, we can handle it as a propositional statement as in the previous section. This means we can analyse it using truth tables or manipulate it using the proof rules.

The symbols $\exists$ and $\forall$ are logical quantifiers. $\forall$ means the statement is true when it is instantiated with any element of the domain. $\exists$ means the statement is true when it is instantiated with some elements of the domain. In this sense, $\exists$ is less committing than $\forall$. For example, consider a domain of days of the week, The following captures the commitment that John Major works every day of the week. This second commitment could be as low as one day of the week and still be true.

$$\forall X \; john\text{-}major\text{-}works(X)$$

Whereas, the following captures the commitment that John Major works some days of the week.

$$\exists X \; john\text{-}major\text{-}works(X)$$

In order to ascertain whether a $\forall$ statement is true, we have to show it is true for any element of the domain, whereas to show $\exists$ is true, we have to show it is true for at least one element of the domain. Consider the following examples. The first and second are true, and the third and fourth are false.

$$\forall X \; has\text{-}london\text{-}address(X) \rightarrow has\text{-}uk\text{-}address(X)$$

$$\exists X \; has\text{-}london\text{-}address(X) \land has\text{-}hollywood\text{-}address(X)$$

$$\forall X \; has\text{-}london\text{-}address(X) \rightarrow has\text{-}hollywood\text{-}address(X)$$

$$\exists X \; perpetual\text{-}motion\text{-}machine(X)$$

We can extend the proof theory of classical propositional logic to give a proof theory for classical predicate logic, by adding proof rules for the quantifiers (Table 2.7). Using these proof rules, consider the following example of universal elimination.

$$has\text{-}london\text{-}address(john\text{-}major)$$

$$\forall X \; has\text{-}london\text{-}address(X) \rightarrow has\text{-}uk\text{-}address(X)$$

Then by instantiation, the quantified formula becomes,

$$has\text{-}london\text{-}address(john\text{-}major) \rightarrow has\text{-}uk\text{-}address(john\text{-}major)$$

Then by implies elimination, we get *has-uk-address(john-major)*. As another example of using these proof rules, consider the following statement.

$$\forall X \; votes(X, john)$$

Here for all the elements of the domain, say people, they vote for john. From this, we can derive the following.

$$\exists Y \; \forall \; X \; votes(X, Y)$$

This is a more general statement, saying that there is some element of the domain, a person who all the people vote for. This is an example of exists introduction.

23

∀ Introduction	If we can derive α, then we can derive $\forall X\ \beta$, where β is obtained from α by replacing every occurrence of some constant by X, and this constant is not used in the assumptions.
∀ Elimination (Instantiation)	If we can derive $\forall X\ \alpha$, then we can derive β, where β is obtained from α by replacing every occurrence of X by some constant.
∃ Introduction	If we can derive α, then we can derive $\exists X\ \beta$, where β is obtained from α by replacing every occurrence of some constant by X.
∃ Elimination (Instantiation)	If we can derive $\exists X\ \alpha$, then we can derive β, where β is obtained from α by replacing every occurrence of X by some constant, and this constant is not used in the assumptions.

Table 2.7: Proof rules for quantifiers

2.3.3 Classical set theory

Closely related to classical logic is classical set theory. Whilst the concepts are widely known, we briefly review in Table 2.8 operations on sets. In Table 2.9, we present some key laws for handling set theory statements.

Many types of information can be easily and naturally handled using set theory. For example, consider the following information about names and addresses.

$Names = \{john\text{-}smith, ann\text{-}green, blogg\&co,$
$\qquad\qquad acme\text{-}widgets, bengal\text{-}restaurant, happy\text{-}bank, \ldots\ldots\}$

The residential and business names are subsets of the set of names.

$$Residential\text{-}Names = \{john\text{-}smith, ann\text{-}green, ...\}$$

$$Business\text{-}Names = \{blogg\&co, acme\text{-}widgets,$$
$$bengal\text{-}restaurant, happy\text{-}bank, ...\}$$

Also, consider addresses.

$$Addresses = \{24high\text{-}street, 6meadow\text{-}drive, mega\text{-}towers, ...\}$$

A Cartesian product allows us to form a set of tuples from two or more sets of information. For example, we can associate names with addresses by taking the Cartesian product of *Names* and *Addresses* as follows.

$$Names \times Addresses = \{(john\text{-}smith, 24high\text{-}street),$$
$$(john\text{-}smith, 6meadow\text{-}drive),$$
$$(john\text{-}smith, mega\text{-}towers),$$
$$(ann\text{-}green, 24high\text{-}street), ...\}$$

The actual set of names and addresses, denoted *Names&Addresses* will be a subset of the above. From this, we might be interested in the set of residential names and addresses. This we can form from the above as follows.

Residential-Names&Addresses
$= \{(X, Y) \mid X \in Residential\text{-}Names$ and $(X, Y) \in Names\&Addresses\}$

Here the pair (X, Y) is in the set *Residential-Names&Addresses* if X is in *Residential-Names* and (X, Y) is in *Names&Addresses*. In this way, we are forming new sets from other sets. This feature together with the powerful operations, over sets and useful properties and equivalences, means that classical set theory is readily applicable to modelling and reasoning within information systems. For example, relational algebra for database systems, and specification formalisms such as Z for systems engineering, are based directly on classical set theory.

Note the parallel between the laws for set theory in Table 2.9 and those for classical logic. If we treat sets as representing propositions, and we swop disjunction for union, conjunction for intersection, and negation for complementation, then these laws hold for classical logic. For example the following hold.

25

Subset	The set A is a subset of the set B, denoted $A \subseteq B$, if every element of A is in B.
Complementation	The complement of set A, denoted $\overline{A}$, is the set of items not in A. This is usually with respect to some explicit domain.
Union	The union of sets A and B, denoted $A \cup B$, is the set of elements which belong to either A or B.
Intersection	The intersection of sets A and B, denoted $A \cap B$, is the set of elements that belong to both A and B.
Difference	The difference of set A with set B, denoted $A - B$, is the set of elements that belong to A but not to B.
Product	The Cartesian product of sets A and B, denoted $A \times B$, is the set of pairs (r, s) where r is in A and s is in B.

Table 2.8: Operations on sets

De Morgan's Laws	$\overline{A \cup B} = \overline{A} \cap \overline{B}$ $\overline{A \cap B} = \overline{A} \cup \overline{B}$
Distributive Laws	$C \cap (A \cup B) = (C \cap A) \cup (C \cap B)$ $C \cup (A \cap B) = (C \cup A) \cap (C \cup B)$

Table 2.9: Laws for handling set theory statements

$$\neg(A \lor B) = \neg A \land \neg B$$

$$C \land (A \lor B) = (C \land A) \lor (C \land B)$$

Actually, the relationship between classical logic and classical set theory is very close. Indeed in many respects, they can be viewed as equivalent. To illustrate, we briefly consider the relationship between sets and relations. Consider the following set.

$$Primary\text{-}colours = \{red, green, blue\}$$

This set is equivalent to the following relation.

$$primary\text{-}colour(red)$$
$$primary\text{-}colour(green)$$
$$primary\text{-}colour(blue)$$

Similarly, relations greater than unary can be viewed as sets. Consider the following relation.

$$capital\text{-}of(paris, france)$$
$$capital\text{-}of(tokyo, japan)$$
$$\vdots$$

This can be viewed as the following set.

$$Capital\text{-}of = \{(paris, france), (tokyo, japan), ...\}$$

The relationship between sets and relations continues with connectives. Suppose the following two sets indicate our suppliers.

$$Hardware = \{apple, ibm\}$$
$$Software = \{apple, microsoft\}$$

The relations for these are the following.

$$hardware(apple)$$
$$hardware(ibm)$$
$$software(apple)$$
$$software(microsoft)$$

The set of suppliers is then the following union.

$$Suppliers = Hardware \cup Software$$

This can be represented by the following statement.

$$\forall X \; suppliers(X) \leftrightarrow hardware(X) \vee software(X)$$

The relation *suppliers* is therefore the following.

$$suppliers(apple)$$
$$suppliers(ibm)$$
$$suppliers(microsoft)$$

In this way, disjunction and union are equivalent. Suppose, we are now interested in those suppliers that supply both hardware and software.

$$Both = Hardware \cap Software$$

Expressing this in logic can be achieved by the following.

$$\forall X \; both(X) \leftrightarrow hardware(X) \wedge software(X)$$

The relation *both* is therefore *both(apple)*. In this way, conjunction and intersection are equivalent. We can show further equivalences between negation and complementation operations, and implication and subset relations.

2.3.4   Classical formalisms and uncertain information

The proof theory of classical logic can be automated [Fit90, Bib93] so that if a set of propositions implies a particular proposition, then we can find a proof for that proposition in a finite number of steps. For propositional logic, and for a useful range of databases for predicate logic, we can also automate the testing of the consistency of a set of propositions. This means we can use classical logic as the basis for information handling. Indeed there are programming languages, database systems, and expert systems tools that are directly based on classical logic.

Classical logic represents some kinds of incomplete information for example by using disjunction. Suppose we want to represent the age of *bill-clinton*, but do not know anything other than he is in his mid-forties.

$$age(bill\text{-}clinton, 44) \vee age(bill\text{-}clinton, 45)$$
$$\vee \; age(bill\text{-}clinton, 46) \vee age(bill\text{-}clinton, 47)$$

Here, we have used disjunction to cover the alternatives. We know one of them is true, but do not know which one. In this way, even though the knowledge is incomplete, it is useful and relevant, and inferences can be derived from it.

Whilst classical formalisms are clearly appropriate for certain kinds of uncertain information, such as disjunctive information and some forms of incomplete information, they are significantly limited for addressing certain key important kinds of uncertainty, such as probabilistic, fuzzy, default and inconsistent information. In the following chapters we cover the problems of handling probabilistic, fuzzy, default and inconsistent information in a classical formalism, and review alternative approaches to formalization.

In general there are many design considerations for formalizing uncertainty including expressiveness of the language, and strength of the system for manipulating statements of the language, i.e., the axiomatization. If an insufficiently expressive language is adopted, then it cannot represent all the information that will be potentially available. Similarly if the power of the reasoning system is weak, then potentially some inferences will be lost. Unfortunately using more expressive languages and using more powerful reasoning systems render the mechanization less computationally viable. Yet to be practical the algorithms that mechanize the reasoning should be computationally viable, otherwise the system will be too frequently paralysed by indecision. To delineate this problem, there are extensive mathematical analyses of computational properties of many of the proposals for handling information.

Chapter 3

Probabilistic Information

3.1 Introduction

Most people have recourse to using probabilistic information at some time. Take betting for instance. In a wide variety of situations, reasoning with probabilistic information can be intuitive, and can provide a powerful means for overcoming uncertainty.

Use of probabilistic information is widespread in organizations. Diverse activities such as engineering design, accounts auditing, production planning, and market research, all involve approximate information. In these kinds of activities, probabilistic information could come from undertaking experiments or surveys. For example, testing mechanical properties of components or asking samples of customers questions on product preference. Alternatively, probabilistic information could come from the subjective analysis of situations. For example, a production planner with a lot of experience might present a plan argued in terms of the probabilities that certain production targets are viable.

Currently, little reasoning with probabilistic information is automated. There are specialist software packages for complex statistical analyses of detailed bodies of data. Such tools might be used by limited numbers of statisticians in specialist roles such as engineering or marketing. But most interpretation of probabilistic information is not automated. Whether probabilities are obtained from large bodies of data or from subjective evaluation, the decisions that are made using the information do not usually involve computer-based reasoning.

However, there are now viable techniques for incorporating computer-based probabilistic reasoning into information technology. We explore the ideas behind these techniques in this chapter and consider applications in later chapters.

3.2   Probability theory

Probability theory is well-established. It provides an intuitive and yet powerful formalization for handling likelihoods. Furthermore, there is a viable and intuitive approach to computing with probabilisitic information, namely Bayesian networks. Here we review some basic well-known features of probability in order to introduce Bayesian networks in section 3.3. For a more comprehensive introduction to probability theory see [Lip65, Fel68], and for general arguments on the applicability of probability theory to artificial intelligence and expert systems see [Lin87, SP90].

3.2.1   Probability

To consider using probabilistic information, we review a few important concepts, including sample space, event probability and conditional probability.

Every conceivable outcome of an experiment, or trial, is an element in the sample space S for that experiment or trial. So if we roll a dice, we could describe the outcome as one element out of the set of possible outcomes $S = \{1, 2, 3, 4, 5, 6\}$. Similarly, if we toss a coin twice, then we are considering a sample space $\{hh, ht, th, tt\}$, where hh denotes two heads uppermost, ht denotes heads followed by tails, and so on.

An event, denoted α, is a subset of the sample space S. An event "occurs" if the outcome is an element of α. For example, an event α is the event that when a coin is tossed twice, the first toss is a head, $\{hh, ht\}$. Similarly, an event β is the event that when a coin is tossed twice, at least one head turns upwards, $\{ht, hh, th\}$.

Associated with each point α in the sample space S is a non-negative number, called the probability of α, and is denoted $P(\alpha)$. The sum of all probabilities for the points in S is 1. For example, if we assume that for the dice, each outcome is equally possible, then the probability of each outcome is $1/6$. Hence, the following holds,

$$P(1) + P(2) + P(3) + P(4) + P(5) + P(6) = 1$$

Given an event α, the probability of the event is $P(\alpha)$, and is the sum of the probabilities of all the sample points in it. Since the probability of the whole sample space is 1, then the probability of any event α is such that the following holds,

$$0 \leq P(\alpha) \leq 1$$

For example if a coin is tossed twice, we can assign equal probabilities to each of the four possible outcomes for the two tosses of the coin, then

$$P(hh) = P(ht) = P(th) = P(tt) = 1/4$$

So the probability α that the first toss is heads is the following.

$$P(\alpha) = P(hh) + P(ht) = 1/2$$

Similarly we can calculate the probability that at least one head turns upwards is as follows.

$$P(\alpha) = P(hh) + P(ht) + P(th) = 3/4$$

We can now consider how to combine probabilities for different events. First, an event β is said to be independent of an event α, if the probability that β occurs is not influenced by whether α has or has not occurred. If the probability of an event α is $P(\alpha)$, and the probability of β is $P(\beta)$, and α and β are independent events, then the probability $P(\alpha \wedge \beta)$ is as follows.

$$P(\alpha \wedge \beta) = P(\alpha).P(\beta)$$

So for example, let α be the event that when a dice is rolled, an even number is uppermost, and let β be the event that when a coin is tossed twice, there is at least one head turned uppermost. Let the following be their probabilities.

$$P(\alpha) = 1/2$$

$$P(\beta) = 3/4$$

Since α and β are independent events, then the probability that both events occur is as follows.

$$P(\alpha \wedge \beta) = 3/8$$

33

For the complement of an event α, denoted $\neg\alpha$, the probability is as follows.

$$P(\neg\alpha) = 1 - P(\alpha)$$

So for an event α, the probability of it occurring and the probability of it not occurring sum to 1. For example, the probability that $\neg\beta$ is the event that heads does not turn upwards at least once is then the following.

$$P(\neg\beta) = 1/4$$

If the probability of an event α is $P(\alpha)$ and the probability of an event β is $P(\beta)$, then the probability that either occurs, denoted $\alpha \vee \beta$, is as follows.

$$P(\alpha \vee \beta) = P(\alpha) + P(\beta) - P(\alpha \wedge \beta)$$

For example, suppose we toss a gold coin, and a silver coin. Let α be the event that the gold coin turns heads upwards, and let β be the event that the silver coin turns heads upwards. The probability that event α or the event β occurs is $P(\alpha \vee \beta)$. This is $((1/2 + 1/2) - (1/4))$, which is $3/4$. Another view of this probability is the following.

$$P(\alpha \vee \beta) = P(\alpha \wedge \beta) + P(\neg\alpha \wedge \beta) + P(\alpha \wedge \neg\beta)$$

Since the sample space is $\alpha \wedge \beta$, $\neg\alpha \wedge \beta$, $\alpha \wedge \neg\beta$ and $\neg\alpha \wedge \neg\beta$, and each of these options is equally probable. So $P(\alpha \vee \beta)$ is $3 \times (1/4)$, which is $3/4$.

In this section, whilst we have defined events as sets, we have viewed them as propositions. Hence, instead of using the set-theoretic symbols for intersection, union, and complementation, we have used the logic symbols for conjunction, disjunction and negation respectively.

3.2.2 Conditional probability

Conditional probability is the probability of a particular event, given the probability of another specific event. For example, suppose we have two containers, a red one and a blue one. The red container contains two black balls and three white balls. The blue container contains one black and one white ball. Suppose a container is chosen at random and a ball chosen from it. The sample space is as follows.

$$red\text{-}container \land black\text{-}ball$$
$$red\text{-}container \land white\text{-}ball$$
$$blue\text{-}container \land black\text{-}ball$$
$$blue\text{-}container \land white\text{-}ball$$

The first item in this list means a black ball from the red container has been selected. The rest can be interpreted similarly. For this example, we know the following probabilities.

$$P(red\text{-}container) = 1/2$$
$$P(blue\text{-}container) = 1/2$$

We also know information such as the probability of "selecting a black ball given that we have selected the red container" is 2/5. To adopt a standard notation, we represent this by the following, where the notation "|" means that the item on the left of the symbol is conditional on the item on the right.

$$P(black\text{-}ball \mid red\text{-}container) = 2/5$$

Using this notation, we have, in addition, the following conditional probabilities.

$$P(white\text{-}ball \mid red\text{-}container) = 3/5$$
$$P(black\text{-}ball \mid blue\text{-}container) = 1/2$$
$$P(white\text{-}ball \mid blue\text{-}container) = 1/2$$

In this example, the probability of selecting a black ball from the red container is the probability of selecting a black ball from the red container given that we have the red container i.e. 2/5, multiplied by the probability of selecting a ball from the red container, i.e. 1/2.

$$P(red\text{-}container \land black\text{-}ball)$$
$$= P(red\text{-}container).P(black\text{-}ball \mid red\text{-}container)$$
$$= (1/2).(2/5)$$
$$= 1/5$$

Similarly,

$$P(blue\text{-}container \land white\text{-}ball)$$
$$= P(blue\text{-}container).P(white\text{-}ball \mid blue\text{-}container)$$
$$= (1/2).(1/2)$$
$$= 1/4$$

35

In general, for any events the following holds.

$$P(\alpha \wedge \beta) = P(\alpha).P(\beta \mid \alpha)$$

Conditional probabilities can form the basis for using probabilistic information in information systems, as we indicate in the following subsection.

3.2.3   Conditional probabilities in information systems

Conditional probabilities can be used to represent contingent information. If e denotes evidence, and h denotes some hypothesis, then the statement $P(h|e)$ denotes the probability of the hypothesis given the evidence. This form can then naturally be used for diagnostic or predictive knowledge representation, such as the following.

$$P(rain \mid dark\text{-}clouds) = 0.5$$

$$P(flat\text{-}battery \mid car\text{-}does\text{-}not\text{-}start \wedge headlights\text{-}do\text{-}not\text{-}work) = 0.9$$

However, using conditional probabilities directly is problematical since much information is required. Indeed, we really need a probability value for every combination of events in the sample space. This is called a total (probability) distribution.

Suppose we have two independent events α and β. Then we need to know three from the following probabilities for a total distribution. Each of these combinations is a joint probability. A total distribution in this form is called a joint distribution.

$$P(\alpha \wedge \beta)$$
$$P(\alpha \wedge \neg\beta)$$
$$P(\neg\alpha \wedge \beta)$$
$$P(\neg\alpha \wedge \neg\beta)$$

This gives us four joint probabilities to use since they all add to 1. If we have three independent events, then we use eight joint probabilities. If we have four independent events, then we use sixteen joint probabilities. To generalize, if we have n independent events, then we use 2^n joint probabilities. Since, we have the following.

$$P(\alpha \wedge \beta) = P(\alpha).P(\beta \mid \alpha)$$

We can also present a probability distribution by conditional probabilities. So for two independent events α and β, the following conditional probabilities are sufficient for a total distribution.

$$P(\alpha \mid \beta)$$
$$P(\alpha \mid \neg\beta)$$
$$P(\beta)$$

One of the key objections to using probability theory is that the complete specification of a total distribution requires many conditional probability statements, or equivalently joint probabilities.

To ameliorate this problem, we can adopt assumptions about certain propositions being mutually independent. As we stated earlier, two propositions are independent if the value of one has no effect on the value of the other. So α is independent of β given γ if the following holds.

$$P(\alpha \mid \beta \wedge \gamma) = P(\alpha \mid \gamma)$$

In other words, adding β to γ makes no difference to the probability of α given γ. Note, it is also possible that the following situation holds.

$$P(\alpha \mid \beta \wedge \gamma) = P(\alpha \mid \gamma)$$
$$P(\alpha \mid \beta \wedge \gamma \wedge \delta) \neq P(\alpha \mid \beta \wedge \gamma)$$

So, independence depends on the combination of propositions involved. By assuming independence between some of the propositions, we can decrease the number of conditional probability statements required. This issue is explored more in the section on Bayesian networks (Section 3.3).

3.2.4 Axioms of probability theory

In this section, we consolidate the ideas presented so far in this chapter in the form of the axioms of probability theory. We have based our definition on events, which are subsets of the sample space.

Let S be a sample space, let E be the set of events, and let P be a function that maps elements of E to a number in the range 0 to 1 satisfying the following three conditions.

37

1. For every event α, $0 \leq P(\alpha) \leq 1$.

2. $P(S) = 1$.

3. If $\alpha_1, ..., \alpha_n$ is a sequence of mutually exclusive events, i.e. non-intersecting subsets of S

$$P(\alpha_1 \vee ... \vee \alpha_n) = P(\alpha_1) + ... + P(\alpha_n)$$

In addition we assume the definition of conditional probability $P(\alpha \mid \beta)$, as follows, where $P(\beta) \neq 0$.

$$P(\alpha \mid \beta) = \frac{P(\alpha \wedge \beta)}{P(\beta)}$$

As a direct result of these definitions, we obtain axioms such as the following. First, any conditional probability is a number between 0 and 1.

$$0 \leq P(\alpha \mid \beta) \leq 1$$

Second, the probability of an event plus the probability of its negation is always 1. In other words, either an event or its negation is true. This is similar to $\alpha \vee \neg\alpha$ being always true in classical logic.

$$P(\alpha \mid \beta) + P(\neg\alpha \mid \beta) = 1$$

Third, if the event α is a subset of event β, then $P(\alpha) \leq P(\beta)$ holds. Fourth, if α and β are any two events, then the following holds.

$$P(\alpha \vee \beta) = P(\alpha) + P(\beta) - P(\alpha \wedge \beta)$$

For conjunction, we can derive the following generalization, called the multiplication theorem, using the axioms of probability.

$P(\alpha_1 \wedge \alpha_2 \wedge ... \wedge \alpha_n)$
    $= P(\alpha_1)P(\alpha_2 \mid \alpha_1).P(\alpha_3 \mid \alpha_1 \wedge \alpha_2)...P(\alpha_n \mid \alpha_1 \wedge \alpha_2 \wedge ...\alpha_{n-1})$

We use this generalization for reasoning in Bayesian networks.

3.2.5 Subjective versus objective views of probability

Two ways of obtaining probabilistic information are described as subjective and objective. In the objective approach, a number of examples are used to calculate the frequency that an event occurs out of the possible events. For example, the probability that a coin will turn up heads is the proportion of events that this outcome occurs. In a practical setting, this will usually be close to 1/2, if enough examples of tosses are used.

By contrast, the subjective approach is based on the degree of belief that the user has in an event occurring. So for the event that a coin will turn up heads, most users would represent their belief that the event would occur by the ratio 1/2. Though, if they know other information about the coin such as it had heads on both sides, then they would offer the probability of 1. Hence, the degree of belief a user has in a proposition is context sensitive.

The subjective view can be motivated by considering its application in betting. Suppose a user is betting on an ordinary coin turning up heads. If the gamble is such that for a bet of $1, the user gets $2 in return, then it would be reasonable to expect the user to not lose money over a number of gambles. But, if the proportion of the number of heads falls below 1/2, then the user will lose money. Whereas if the ratio goes above 1/2, the user will gain money. This is called the Dutch book argument.

3.3 Bayesian networks

Bayesian networks are an approach to using conditional probabilities in information systems [Pea86, Pea87, LS88, HW95]. By augmenting the use of conditional probabilities with extra structural information, they are more efficient for representing and reasoning with probabilistic information. In particular they incorporate assumptions about which propositions are independent of other propositions, thereby simplifying the computations.

They are used to model situations in which causality, or influence is prevalent, but in which we only have a partial understanding, hence the need to model probabilistically.

Essentially, probabilistic networks are a set of nodes with directed arcs (arrows) providing connections between nodes. Every node is connected to another node, but each node is not necessarily connected to every other node. Each node denotes a random variable, which is a variable that can be instantiated with an element from the sample space for the variable. In this chapter, we assume random variables for events that are either "true" or "false". For example, if the random variable is *car-battery-is-flat*, then this variable can be instantiated with the event *car-battery-is-flat*, or the event ¬*car-battery-is-flat*.

3.3.1 Identifying independence assumptions

As discussed earlier, α and β are independent if $P(\alpha \mid \beta) = P(\alpha)$. So for example, if α and β are independent, then β does not need to be considered in calculating the probability of α. Independence assumptions are intuitive and can be used widely.

In order to indicate how the structural information is used, we consider three simple types of network, namely converging, diverging, and linear. Each represents different independence assumptions. We show how these can be used to simplify reasoning with conditional probability statements.

Converging Consider the converging network in Figure 3.1. This is called converging because the arrows converge on one of the nodes.

Figure 3.1: A converging network

Suppose α denotes "car engine stalls", β denotes "fuel tank is empty", and γ denotes "electrical failure". So either β or γ will cause α to hold. β and γ are conditionally independent: If we don't know whether α holds, then the belief in β is independent of γ. If we know α holds, then this can affect our belief in β and in γ. Hence, β and γ are conditionally dependent, given α. For this network, we have the following.

$$P(\alpha \wedge \beta \wedge \gamma) = P(\alpha \mid \beta \wedge \gamma).P(\beta \mid \gamma).P(\gamma)$$

However, since β and γ are independent, then we have the following.

$$P(\beta \mid \gamma) = P(\beta)$$

Hence, we can reduce the above to the following.

$$P(\alpha \wedge \beta \wedge \gamma) = P(\alpha \mid \beta \wedge \gamma).P(\beta).P(\gamma)$$

We can't reduce this anymore. In a similar way, we can calculate $P(\alpha \wedge \beta \wedge \neg\gamma)$, $P(\alpha \wedge \neg\beta \wedge \gamma)$, $P(\alpha \wedge \neg\beta \wedge \neg\gamma)$, $P(\neg\alpha \wedge \beta \wedge \gamma)$, $P(\neg\alpha \wedge \beta \wedge \neg\gamma)$, $P(\neg\alpha \wedge \neg\beta \wedge \gamma)$, and $P(\neg\alpha \wedge \neg\beta \wedge \neg\gamma)$.

Diverging Consider the diverging network in Figure 3.2. This is called diverging because the arrows diverge from α.

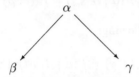

Figure 3.2: A diverging network

Suppose α denotes "car battery is flat", β denotes "car does not start", and γ denotes "lights do not work". Suppose we know α, then knowing β has no effect on γ, and vice versa. Hence β and γ are conditionally independent given α, though they are not independent. For this network we have the following.

$$
\begin{aligned}
P(\alpha \wedge \beta \wedge \gamma) &= P(\alpha \mid \beta \wedge \gamma).P(\beta \mid \gamma).P(\gamma) \\
&= P(\gamma \mid \beta \wedge \alpha).P(\beta \mid \alpha).P(\alpha)
\end{aligned}
$$

Since β and γ are independent given α, we have the following.

$$P(\gamma \mid \beta \wedge \alpha) = P(\gamma \mid \alpha)$$

Hence, we can obtain the following.

$$P(\alpha \wedge \beta \wedge \gamma) = P(\gamma \mid \alpha).P(\beta \mid \alpha).P(\alpha)$$

We can't reduce this anymore. Note how this reduction, and the assumptions used to generate it, differ from the converging case.

Linear Consider the linear network in Figure 3.3. Suppose α denotes "engine overheating", β denotes "low-water level in the cooling system", and γ denotes "leaking hose pipe in the cooling system". Suppose we know α, then this may change the belief in β. However, once we know β, changes in the belief of α do not affect the belief in γ causing β. Hence α and γ are conditionally independent given β. For this network we have the following.

$$P(\alpha \wedge \beta \wedge \gamma) = P(\alpha \mid \beta \wedge \gamma).P(\beta \mid \gamma).P(\gamma)$$

Since, α and γ are independent given β, then we have the following.

$$P(\alpha \mid \beta \wedge \gamma) = P(\alpha \mid \beta)$$

Hence, we have the following.

$$P(\alpha \wedge \beta \wedge \gamma) = P(\alpha \mid \beta).P(\beta \mid \gamma).P(\gamma)$$

We can't reduce this anymore. Note, how even though both the diverging and linear cases are based on two nodes being conditionally independent given the third node, the form of the reduced probability statement is different.

Figure 3.3: A linear network

By repeated application of these three cases, independence assumptions can be identified in larger networks. From this, the total probability distribution for a large set of propositions may be represented by a relatively small number of explicit conditional probabilities. We use this approach in the following section.

3.3.2 Reasoning in Bayesian networks

In order to illustrate how we can use Bayesian networks, we consider the following example taken from [Coo84], and base the explanation on [Spi86a]. The example is based on the following piece of medical knowledge.

> "Metastatic cancer is a possible cause of a brain tumour, and is also an explanation for increased serum calcium. In turn, either of these could explain a patient falling into a coma. Severe headaches are also possibly associated with a brain tumour."

This knowledge can be represented by the causal model in Figure 3.4, where α denotes "metastatic cancer", β denotes "increased total serum calcium", γ denotes "brain tumour", δ denotes "coma", and ε denotes "severe headaches".

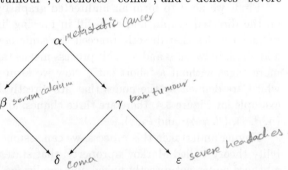

Figure 3.4: Bayesian network where α denotes metastatic cancer, β denotes increased total serum calcium, γ denotes brain tumour, δ denotes coma, and ε severe headaches.

The joint distribution for the random variables $\alpha, \beta, \gamma, \delta$ and ε is such that the following holds.

$$P(\alpha \wedge \beta \wedge \gamma \wedge \delta \wedge \varepsilon)$$
$$= P(\varepsilon \mid \alpha \wedge \beta \wedge \gamma \wedge \delta).P(\delta \mid \alpha \wedge \beta \wedge \gamma).P(\gamma \mid \alpha \wedge \beta).P(\beta \mid \alpha).P(\alpha)$$

Using the Bayesian network in Figure 3.4, this can be simplified to the following.

$$= P(\varepsilon \mid \delta).P(\delta \mid \beta \wedge \gamma).P(\gamma \mid \alpha).P(\beta \mid \alpha).P(\alpha)$$

This can be obtained from the following set of conditional probabilities.

$$P(\varepsilon \mid \gamma) \qquad P(\varepsilon \mid \neg\gamma)$$
$$P(\delta \mid \beta \wedge \gamma) \qquad P(\delta \mid \beta \wedge \neg\gamma)$$
$$P(\delta \mid \neg\beta \wedge \gamma) \qquad P(\delta \mid \neg\beta \wedge \neg\gamma)$$
$$P(\beta \mid \alpha) \qquad P(\beta \mid \neg\alpha)$$
$$P(\gamma \mid \alpha) \qquad P(\gamma \mid \neg\alpha)$$
$$P(\alpha)$$

When the Bayesian network is used, evidence can be received about any node in the network. However, to be able to propagate evidence through the network, we need some further information. More specifically we need to be able to undertake local computations for updating probabilities through the network. For this, we need to use a simple way of storing the required relationships in an undirected form.

First, we need to form an undirected graph by dropping the directions on the directed graph, and then fill in missing links between each pair of unlinked nodes that directly preceed the same node. So for Figure 3.4, we add a link between β and γ. This process means that there is no cycle of 4 or more edges without a "short cut". Now we form subgraphs, called cliques, which are defined by the nodes that are directly linked to each other. For example for Figure 3.4, there are three cliques, and these are represented by (α, β, γ), (β, γ, δ), and (γ, ε).

Having undertaken this process, we can assume a general result of probability theory, called Markov's property, that states a node is independent of all those nodes not directly linked and conditional on those that are linked. Hence, cliques are useful because the relevant joint distributions can be represented as a simple function of the distributions on the cliques.

Returning to our example above, the joint distribution may be written, as before, as follows, where $\alpha, \beta, \gamma, \delta$ and ε are random variables.

$$P(\alpha\wedge\beta\wedge\gamma\wedge\delta\wedge\varepsilon) = P(\varepsilon \mid \alpha\wedge\beta\wedge\gamma\wedge\delta).P(\delta \mid \alpha\wedge\beta\wedge\gamma).P(\gamma \mid \alpha\wedge\beta).P(\beta \mid \alpha).P(\alpha)$$

By using Markov's property on the undirected graph described above, we rewrite the above equation as follows.

$$= P(\varepsilon \mid \gamma).P(\delta \mid \beta \wedge \gamma).P(\beta \wedge \gamma \mid \alpha).P(\alpha)$$

Then by conditional probability, we rewrite the above equation as follows.

$$= \frac{P(\gamma \wedge \varepsilon)}{P(\gamma)} \quad . \quad \frac{P(\beta \wedge \gamma \wedge \delta)}{P(\beta \wedge \gamma)} \quad . \quad P(\alpha \wedge \beta \wedge \gamma)$$

Clique (α, β, γ)	Clique (β, γ, δ)	Clique (δ, ε)
$P(\alpha \wedge \beta \wedge \gamma)$	$P(\beta \wedge \gamma \wedge \delta)$	$P(\gamma \wedge \varepsilon)$
$P(\alpha \wedge \beta \wedge \neg\gamma)$	$P(\beta \wedge \gamma \wedge \neg\delta)$	$P(\gamma \wedge \neg\varepsilon)$
$P(\alpha \wedge \neg\beta \wedge \gamma)$	$P(\beta \wedge \neg\gamma \wedge \delta)$	$P(\neg\gamma \wedge \varepsilon)$
$P(\alpha \wedge \neg\beta \wedge \neg\gamma)$	$P(\beta \wedge \neg\gamma \wedge \neg\delta)$	$P(\neg\gamma \wedge \neg\varepsilon)$
$P(\neg\alpha \wedge \beta \wedge \gamma)$	$P(\neg\beta \wedge \gamma \wedge \delta)$	
$P(\neg\alpha \wedge \beta \wedge \neg\gamma)$	$P(\neg\beta \wedge \gamma \wedge \neg\delta)$	
$P(\neg\alpha \wedge \neg\beta \wedge \gamma)$	$P(\neg\beta \wedge \neg\gamma \wedge \delta)$	
$P(\neg\alpha \wedge \neg\beta \wedge \neg\gamma)$	$P(\neg\beta \wedge \neg\gamma \wedge \neg\delta)$	

Table 3.1: Probability distributions on the cliques for the example

In this way, the reasoning in the network can be undertaken by just reasoning with the distributions on the cliques. These in turn can be derived from the assessments made on the causal representation, using the independence assumptions as discussed in Section 3.3.1. So for example, the following can be identified for our example in Figure 3.4.

$$P(\alpha \wedge \beta \wedge \gamma) = P(\beta \mid \alpha).P(\gamma \mid \alpha).P(\alpha)$$

Using this approach, it is straightforward to generate the distributions on the cliques for Figure 3.4. For this example, this means identifying values for Table 3.1.

Now suppose our only data on a patient is that he suffers from severe headaches, so ε is true, and that we wish to assess how that affects our belief in him going into a coma, as represented by $P(\delta \mid \varepsilon)$.

To do this we form a new directed graph for evidence propagation, where each node is labelled. First, the evidence node is labelled 1, then at each step, a label is put on the node attached to the maximum number of nodes that are already labelled. Ties are broken at random. For example, we obtain Figure 3.5 using this process.

Suppose we indicate our current belief, given available evidence, by an asterisk. Then $P^*(\gamma) = P(\gamma \mid \varepsilon)$ can be calculated directly from the values for the probabilities (in Table 3.1) for the clique. At the next clique we have the following.

45

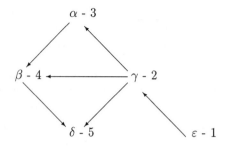

Figure 3.5: Directed graph giving the sequence of nodes to update after having observed ε as being true

$$P^*(\alpha \wedge \beta \wedge \gamma) = P(\alpha \wedge \beta \wedge \gamma \mid \varepsilon)$$

By conditioning, this gives the following.

$$P^*(\alpha \wedge \beta \wedge \gamma) = P(\alpha \wedge \beta \mid \gamma \wedge \varepsilon)$$

Then by using Figure 3.5, we rewrite the above as follows.

$$P^*(\alpha \wedge \beta \wedge \gamma) = P(\alpha \wedge \beta \mid \gamma).P^*(\gamma)$$

By conditioning this gives the following.

$$P^*(\alpha \wedge \beta \wedge \gamma) = \frac{P(\alpha \wedge \beta \wedge \gamma).P^*(\gamma)}{P(\gamma)}$$

A value for $P^*(\alpha \wedge \beta \wedge \gamma)$ can therefore be calculated from the probabilities in Table 3.1. In a similar way, we can calculate $P^*(\alpha \wedge \gamma \wedge \delta)$, which again can be obtained from our current beliefs and the distributions on the cliques. Having propagated the influence of observing ε as true through our graph, we can then calculate the probabilities for $P^*(\alpha)$, $P^*(\beta)$, $P^*(\gamma)$, and in particular $P^*(\delta)$.

This example shows how Bayesian networks can be used to reason with probabilities. Though unfortunately, computation with Bayesian networks is intractable in general [Coo90]. Furthermore, the exponential time limitation does occur on some realistic networks. Some networks as small as ten nodes can take too long, though some networks as large as thousands of nodes can be done in an acceptable time [Cha91]. One solution is to adopt an approximate answer that is likely to be within a small error of the correct answer. Another solution is to adopt algorithms developed for particular topologies or particular queries [HW95].

For more comprehensive introductions to Bayesian networks see [Pea88, Cha91, KC93, SDLC93, HW95]. For more detailed discussion of algorithms for computing with Bayesian networks see [Pea88, LS88, Nea90]. We discuss general issues of applying Bayesian networks to decision-support in Chapter 7, and focus on applying Bayesian networks to information retrieval and information filtering in Chapter 9.

3.4 Outlook for using probabilistic information

Probability theory is well-established, and has significant supporting technology for some applications. For a variety of approaches there is much data that can be used to generate useful reliable conditional probability statements. In addition, probability theory can be applied to a wide range of uncertainty including ignorance (or missing data), linguistic vagueness, and linguistic ambiguity [Hen95].

However, for some applications there might be problems with obtaining reliable probabilities [Nut87], sometimes because not enough is known, and sometimes because of the inherent complexity. They can also be difficult to maintain and expand, given the sensitive nature of interdependencies in probabilistic information.

There might also be problems with desirability. Much information does not come in a probabilistic form, and could be better handled in other ways. For example, heuristics, such as about how foreign exchange rates are affected by government policy, can be useful non-probabilistic information. Whilst it is often possible to force such non-probabilistic information into a probabilistic form, it can cause the information to become less clear, and furthermore may require considerable resources. There is a lively debate on the appropriateness of probability theory for capturing diverse kinds of uncertain information — for example see [Che86, Zad86, Lin87].

Nevertheless Bayesian networks are being used in a variety of applications, including decision-support systems for diagnosis, in particular in medical diagnosis [AWFA87, Cha91], planning [GD95], and in information retrieval [Cro93]. We cover applications in more detail in Chapters 7 and 9.

Whilst Bayesian networks offer an effective way of evaluating the ramifications of evidence on a set of conditional probability statements, they do not allow us to reason with logical statements about probabilistic information. Traditionally, there has been a dichotomy between the probabilistic and logical views of uncertainty in reasoning in artificial intelligence. However, there does seem to be an intuitive overlap of the two views.

By contrast with truth-values in classical logic, probability values are not truth-functional. In classical logic, we can calculate the truth value of $\alpha \wedge \beta$ from the truth value of α and the truth value of β, whereas we cannot calculate the probability of $\alpha \wedge \beta$ from the probability of α and the probability of β. Similarly, in classical logic, we can calculate the truth value of α from the truth value of $\beta \rightarrow \alpha$ and the truth value of β, whereas we cannot calculate the probability of α from the conditional probability $P(\alpha \mid \beta)$ and the probability of β.

Nevertheless, useful logics for reasoning with probabilistic information, probabilistic logics have been proposed [Nil86, Hal90, Bac90]. These logics have been developed to represent information such as "The car probably has some type of malfunction", as follows.

$$P(\exists X \ type\text{-}of\text{-}malfunction(car, X)) > 0.5$$

Another example is "It is more than twice as likely that the car malfunction is electrical rather than the carburettor", which is represented as follows.

$$P(type\text{-}of\text{-}malfunction(car, electrical))$$
$$> 2.P(type\text{-}of\text{-}malfunction(car, carburettor))$$

These logics are based on classical logic extended with notation to represent probabilistic information. Both the proof theory and semantics have been extended to allow inferences to be derived from statements in this extended language.

For a more comprehensive coverage of various approaches to using probability theory, including Bayesian networks and probabilistic logics, see [SP90].

Chapter 4

Fuzzy Information

4.1 Introduction

Most concepts used in human reasoning are to some extent vague or fuzzy. Yet these fuzzy concepts can often be useful because, depending on the context, they can be delineated.

Consider the following example of parking a car taken from [Zad94]. Most people are able to park a car relatively easily. This is partly because the final position of the car and its orientation are not specified precisely in advance of the operation. However, if they were specified precisely, then the difficulty would rise sharply with the degree of precision, until it would be unmanageable for humans. The point of this example is that the task is easy for humans when specified imprecisely and yet difficult to solve by traditional formal methods because such methods do not exploit the tolerance for imprecision. This is highlighted by the following quote from Zadeh [Zad94].

> "The exploitation of the tolerance of imprecision and uncertainty underlies the remarkable human ability to understand distorted speech, decipher sloppy handwriting, comprehend nuances of natural language, summarize text, recognize and classify images, drive a vehicle in dense traffic and, more generally, make rational decisions in an environment of uncertainty and imprecision."

An important aspect of fuzzy reasoning is the ability to handle fuzzy concepts. For example, the ability to know what is meant by tall men, fast cars, or high salaries. Concepts such as men, cars or salaries, can be formalized relatively straightforwardly by techniques based on classical set theory, or classical logic. But, concepts such as tall men, fast cars, or high salaries, are more difficult for classical approaches to model. These concepts are fuzzy, in the sense that they are vague or unclear, and as such require alternative techniques such as offered by the fuzzy systems approach.

Currently, there is much commercial interest in developing and applying systems based on fuzzy sets to control engineering problems. This is partly because fuzzy sets can be used to model systems far more quickly than alternative techniques. Fuzzy control systems can be developed to provide good, though not necessarily optimal solutions, more quickly than traditional control theory. For difficult problems, conventional non-fuzzy methods are usually expensive and depend on mathematical approximations (such as linearization of non-linear problems), which may lead to poor performance. Under such circumstances, fuzzy systems outperform conventional methods [MJ94].

The notion of fuzzy sets has been extended in a number of ways including fuzzy logic, and fuzzy production rules, to give a wide variety of fuzzy systems. In this chapter, we cover some of the basic ideas of fuzzy systems. We start with fuzzy set theory, and then cover a type of fuzzy reasoning called possibilistic reasoning.

4.2 Fuzzy systems

Fuzzy set theory [Zad65], and fuzzy logic [Zad75], have been proposed to handle such fuzzy concepts formally. Fuzzy set theory extends classical set theory. It generalizes the notion of "being in a set", and it generalizes the operations on such sets.

4.2.1 Fuzzy set theory

For a classical set, an item is either in a set or not in it. Often this is described in terms of a membership function as in the following example for the set of even numbers.

$$Evens = \{2, 4, 6, 8, ...\}$$

The membership function for a set returns 0 or 1 for any element in the domain. If it returns 0, it means the element is not in the set. If it returns 1, it means it is in the set. For this we have the membership function defined as follows.

$$f_{Evens}(1) = 0$$
$$f_{Evens}(2) = 1$$
$$f_{Evens}(3) = 0$$
$$f_{Evens}(4) = 1$$

In fuzzy set theory, the notion of a membership function is generalized, so that the degree of membership is graded. In other words, the membership function returns a value between 0 and 1, inclusively. Consider the set of ages that could be described as middle-aged. Here, some ages are clearly in the set such as 45, and to a lesser extent 40 and 50. In addition some might consider 35 and 55 as middle-aged. For this we could have a membership function f_{MA} for the set of ages for middle age, as follows.

$$f_{MA}(30) = 0.0$$
$$f_{MA}(35) = 0.3$$
$$f_{MA}(40) = 0.7$$
$$f_{MA}(45) = 1.0$$
$$f_{MA}(50) = 0.7$$
$$f_{MA}(55) = 0.3$$
$$f_{MA}(60) = 0.0$$

We do not have to restrict the membership function to being discrete. We could have a continuous function. Consider a complete definition for the membership function for ages for middle-age in Figure 4.1.

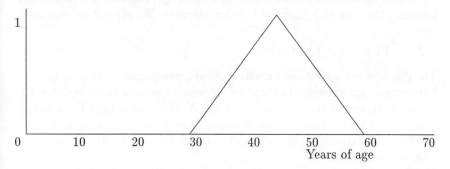

Figure 4.1: A membership function for "middle-age"

Many sets can be naturally and usefully represented using fuzzy membership functions. Consider sets of tall people, sets of large cars, sets of

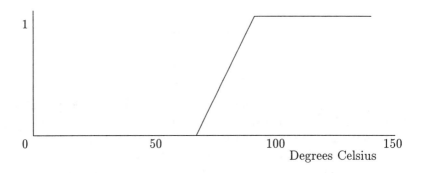

Figure 4.2: A membership function for "hot water"

heavy materials, and so on. These can all be usefully captured by graded membership functions. As another example, consider the membership function for hot water (Figure 4.2). If we denote this function f_{HW}, some values are as follows, where the argument of the function is water temperature in degrees Celsius.

$$f_{HW}(50) = 0.0$$
$$f_{HW}(75) = 0.3$$
$$f_{HW}(95) = 1.0$$

Whilst a fuzzy membership function might appear similar to a probability function, they are very different in other respects. We expand on this later.

4.2.2 Fuzzy set operations

The classical set operations including subset, complementation, union, and intersection, are extended to fuzzy set theory. We present these in Table 4.1, where we represent the domain by the set X. We also require the function $Max(x, y)$ which returns x if x is larger than y and returns y otherwise. Similarly, we require $Min(x, y)$ which returns x if x is smaller than y, and returns y otherwise.

These set theory operations allow us to generalize the classical set theory reasoning discussed in Chapter 2. In addition, principles such as de Morgan's laws and distribution laws also hold for fuzzy set theory. However, unlike classical set theory, the union of a set and its complement does not necessarily equal the domain. Similarly, the intersection of a set and its complement does not necessarily equal the empty set. Clearly, fuzzy set theory reduces to classical set theory when the membership function is restricted to the classical values of 0 and 1.

Subset	The set A is a subset of the set B, denoted $A \subseteq B$, if every x in X, $f_A(x) \leq f_B(x)$, where f_A and f_B are the membership functions for A and B respectively.
Complementation	The complement of set A, denoted $\overline{A}$, is defined by the membership function $f_{\overline{A}}(x)$, where for each x in X, $f_{\overline{A}}(x) = 1 - f_A(x)$.
Union	The union of sets A and B, denoted $A \cup B$, is defined by the membership function $f_{A \cup B}$, where for all x, $f_{A \cup B}(x) = Max(f_A(x), f_B(x))$.
Intersection	The intersection of sets A and B, denoted $A \cap B$, is defined by the function $f_{A \cap B}$, where for all x, $f_{A \cap B} = Min(f_A(x), f_B(x))$.
Equal	The sets A and B are equal, denoted $A = B$, if and only if $f_A(x) = f_B(x)$ for all x in X, where f_A and f_B are the membership functions for A and B respectively.

Table 4.1: Operations on fuzzy sets

To illustrate these definitions, first consider Figure 4.3. Here "infant" is a subset of "young". Now consider the sets in Figure 4.4: the intersection is given in Figure 4.5, and the union in Figure 4.6.

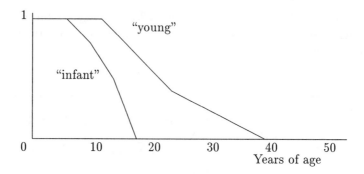

Figure 4.3: Membership functions for "young" and for "infant"

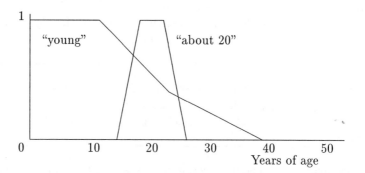

Figure 4.4: Membership functions for "young" and for "about 20"

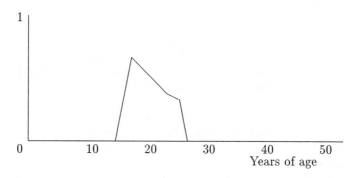

Figure 4.5: Membership function for intersection of "young" and "about 20"

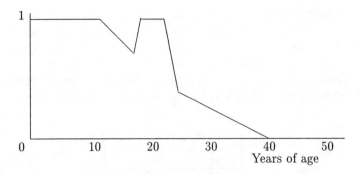

Figure 4.6: Membership function for union of "young" and "about 20"

4.2.3 Fuzzy logic

As discussed in Chapter 2, there is a close relationship between classical logic and classical set theory. This relationship has been used to develop logical counterparts to fuzzy set theory. Here we consider fuzzy logics [Zad75].

The development of fuzzy logics has resulted in two stages of fuzzification. The first is allowing predicates to represent fuzzy sets. The second is to allow for the fuzzification of the notion of truth. For this, the notion of truth is extended from the classical *true* and *false* to a range of truth values such as the following.

$$true$$
$$more\ or\ less\ true$$
$$rather\ true$$
$$not\ very\ true$$
$$not\ very\ false$$
$$\vdots$$
$$false$$

In classical logic, *true* is often represented by the value 1 and *false* by the value 0. Hence *true* = 1 − *false*. To incorporate the spectrum of fuzzy truth values into a fuzzy reasoning system, the fuzzy truth values are defined as a function of each other. So given some value for *true*, we can, for example, define the following.

$$false = 1 - true$$
$$rather\ true = true^2$$

To simplify our exposition, we restrict the coverage to propositional fuzzy logics. We assume the language of classical propositional logic such as α, $\alpha \wedge \beta$, $\beta \rightarrow (\gamma \wedge \delta)$, etc., but use different truth tables to account for the extra truth values. First we consider a simple example that is based on three values *true*, *half-true*, and *false*. For this consider the following truth tables (Tables 4.2 to 4.5) for the connectives [Luk67].

α	$\neg\alpha$
true	*false*
half-true	*half-true*
false	*true*

Table 4.2: Truth table for negation

$\wedge$	*true*	*half-true*	*false*
true	*true*	*half-true*	*false*
half-true	*half-true*	*half-true*	*false*
false	*false*	*false*	*false*

Table 4.3: Truth table for conjunction

$\rightarrow$	*true*	*half-true*	*false*
true	*true*	*half-true*	*false*
half-true	*true*	*true*	*half-true*
false	*true*	*true*	*true*

Table 4.4: Truth table for implication

$\vee$	*true*	*half-true*	*false*
true	*true*	*true*	*true*
half-true	*true*	*half-true*	*half-true*
false	*true*	*half-true*	*false*

Table 4.5: Truth table for disjunction

To illustrate using these truth tables, consider the truth tables of α is *true* and β is *half-true*. For this, $\alpha \wedge \beta$ is *half-true*, $\alpha \to \beta$ is *half-true*, and $\alpha \vee \beta$ is true. Now consider α is *half-true* and β is *false*. For this, $\alpha \wedge \beta$ is *false*, $\alpha \to \beta$ is *half-true*, and $\alpha \vee \beta$ is *half-true*.

Whilst the truth tables for negation, conjunction, and disjunction are widely acceptable interpretations for the notion of *half-true*, the truth table for implication is more difficult to explain. Central to this truth table definition is the desire to force the formula $\alpha \to \alpha$ to be *true* even if α is *half-true*.

These truth tables can be generalized to many values by the following definition from Łukasiewicz where the function *value* returns a truth value in the range 0 to 1, such that 0 is *false*, 1/2 is *half-true*, and 1 is *true*.

$$value(\neg \alpha) = 1 - value(\alpha)$$

$$value(\alpha \wedge \beta) = Min(value(\alpha), value(\beta))$$

$$value(\alpha \vee \beta) = Max(value(\alpha), value(\beta))$$

$$value(\alpha \to \beta) = 1 \text{ if } value(\alpha) \leq value(\beta)$$

$$value(\alpha \to \beta) = 1 - (value(\alpha) + value(\beta)) \text{ if } value(\alpha) > value(\beta)$$

Other definitions for the function *value* provide different fuzzy logics. An alternative definition for implication is the following Kleene-Dienes implication [Die49].

$$Max(1 - value(\alpha), value(\beta))$$

The class of fuzzy logics therefore provides a range of approaches for logical reasoning with fuzzy information. For a review of these options see [DP88a, KGK94].

Fuzzy logics can also be viewed as a form of many-valued logics. Many-valued logics have been proposed as a way to increase the number of truth values from two to three, four or many truth values. For three valued logic, various motivations have been made for the third value. These have included attempts to capture notions such as unknown, possible, and undecidable. In Chapter 4, we discuss four-valued logic, where the extra truth values are *neither true nor false* and *both true and false*, that has been proposed for reasoning with inconsistent information. However, in general, the intuitions behind the truth values for many-valued logics overlap with those for fuzzy logics.

4.3 Possibilistic reasoning

Possibilistic reasoning can be viewed as an analogue of probabilistic reasoning. In probabilistic reasoning, every item in the sample space has an associated probability value, and similarly, in possibility theory, every item in the sample space has an associated possibility value. However, possibility theory and probability theory differ in many other respects. We return to this issue later.

For an event α, a possibility value of 0 means that the event is impossible, whereas a possibility value of 1 means that the event is completely possible. Any intermediate value indicates partial possibility.

Fuzzy membership functions can be used as possibility distributions [Zad75]. So considering Figure 4.1, the possibility of a 10 year old or a 20 year old being considered middle-aged is zero. But, after 30 years the possibility rises until 45 years where the possibility is 1. The possibility then decreases until 60 where it is 0 again.

In this section, we introduce some basic notions underlying possibility theory and then explain how it can be used for representing and reasoning with uncertain information. A good comprehensive introduction to possibilistic reasoning is [KGK94].

4.3.1 Possibility theory

A possibility distribution Q is a mapping from a reference set (or sample space as used in probability theory) R to a number in the range 0 to 1, and for which there is at least one element α in R such that $Q(\alpha) = 1$ holds.

First, we require the function $sup(A)$, which returns the highest number in A, or returns 0 when A is an empty set, and $inf(A)$, which returns the lowest number in A, or returns 1 when A is an empty set.

Let R be a sample space. For a possibility distribution Q, a possibility measure, denoted $Poss_Q(A)$ is defined as follows.

$$Poss_Q(A) = sup(\{Q(\alpha) \mid \alpha \in A\})$$

A necessity measure on Q, denoted $Nec_Q(A)$ is defined as follows.

$$Nec_Q(A) = inf(\{1 - Q(\alpha) \mid \alpha \in (R - A)\})$$

The necessity measure can be understood as a certainty measure. Consider the example of the membership function for middle-age (Figure 4.1). For this sample space is the set of natural numbers $\{1, 2, .., 70\}$. Let A be the set $\{40, 41, .., 50\}$, and Q is defined by the pyramidal-shaped graph. So for example, $Q(30) = 0, Q(37) = 0.5$, and $Q(45) = 1$. The choice of A means that $Poss_Q(A) = 1$ and $Nec_Q(A) = 1/3$. This therefore means that it is completely possible that α is actually in A, but it is only partially necessary. In this way, we can get an ordering over events, where some events are more possible than others, and similarly some events are more necessary than others.

For all possibility distributions, the following relationships are easy to show, where R is a sample space, and $A \subseteq R$ holds.

$$Poss_Q(\emptyset) = Nec_Q(\emptyset) = 0$$

$$Poss_Q(R) = Nec_Q(R) = 1$$

$$Nec_Q(A) \leq Poss_Q(A)$$

This can be extended to contradictory events. The following are also derivable from the above definitions for $Poss_Q$ and Nec_Q.

$$Max(Poss_Q(A), Poss_Q(\overline{A})) = 1$$

$$Min(Nec_Q(A), Nec_Q(\overline{A})) = 0$$

$$Poss_Q(A) = 1 - Nec_Q(\overline{A})$$

Hence to continue the above example, if $Poss_Q(A) = 1$, and $Nec_Q(A) = 1/3$, then $Nec_Q(\overline{A}) = 0$, and $Poss_Q(\overline{A}) = 2/3$.

In addition, we can show, and hence use, the following relationships between possibility and necessity measures over sets and the union and intersection of them.

$$Poss_Q(A \cup B) = Max(Poss_Q(A), Poss_Q(B))$$

$$Poss_Q(A \cap B) \leq Min(Poss_Q(A), Poss_Q(B))$$

59

$$Nec_Q(A \cap B) = Min(Nec_Q(A), Nec_Q(B))$$

$$Nec_Q(A \cup B) \geq Max(Nec_Q(A), Nec_Q(B))$$

Since classical set theory is a special case of fuzzy set theory, classical membership functions can be used to define possibility distributions. For example, consider an automatic lighting control system that switches a light on at 18.00 and switches it off at 06.00 every day all year. The membership function in Figure 4.7 is therefore either 1 or 0, according to whether the light is on or off, respectively. If we look at the light at some point during the day, then what is the possibility of the light being on? If we look during the period $A = \{04.00, .., 22.00\}$, then $Poss_Q(A) = 1$, and $Nec_Q(A) = 0$. Hence, it is completely possible the light will be on during the period A, but not necessarily so.

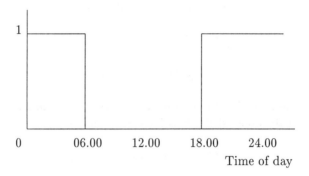

Figure 4.7: Membership function for "light on" in a lighting control system

Whilst there are similarities between possibility theory and probability theory, they do differ in fundamental ways. The basic postulates of the two theories are different. For probability theory, the assignments to each of the events in the sample space should add to exactly 1. This contrasts with possibility theory where the assignments do not have to add to 1.

Using this difference, possibility theory has been proposed as a formalism for representing and reasoning about ignorance or incompleteness. Its proponents argue that in probability theory, ignorance is wrongly interpreted as randomness, where outcomes are equally probable. However, the state of knowledge where there is an equal lack of certainty about all events that are liable to occur cannot be expressed by a single probability measure.

In contrast, possibility theory captures states of knowledge from complete information to total ignorance [DP88a].

Consider the outcomes of rolling an ordinary dice. An equiprobability of 1/6 for each of the possible outcomes expresses the dice is conforming to the behaviour of a normal random dice. In contrast, an equipossibility of 1 for each of the possible outcomes expresses complete ignorance about each possibility, and furthermore this ignorance is represented in a single value for each possible outcome.

In the next section, we show how we can use possibility theory for reasoning about ignorance about truth values in logic.

4.3.2 Possibilistic logic

Possibilistic logic is for reasoning with uncertainty. We have propositions that are *true* or *false*, but due to the lack of precision of the available information, we can in general only estimate to what extent it is possible or necessary that a proposition is *true*. This contrasts with fuzzy logic where the information is vague or incomplete, but not incorrect. The vagueness leads to propostions with intermediary degrees of truth.

The language of possibilistic logic is the same as that for classical logic. However, the principles for handling information about a formula being *true* or *false* are quite different. The formulae $\alpha, \beta, \ldots$ in a database are assigned possibility measures, denoted $Poss(\alpha)$ or necessity measures, denoted $Nec(\alpha)$. These measures are used to represent the degree of confidence in a formula being *true*. For a formula α, $Nec(\alpha) = 1$ means we are certain that α is *true*, whereas $Poss(\alpha) = 1$ means that it is completely possible that α is *true*. Also $Poss(\alpha) = 0$ means α is *false*, whereas $Nec(\alpha) = 0$, and $Poss(\alpha) = 1$, means we are totally ignorant about the truth or falsity of α.

If α is inconsistent, then $Poss(\alpha) = 0$, since it is impossible that α is true. Furthermore, for any α, $Poss(\alpha) = 1$, or $Poss(\neg\alpha) = 1$. In other words, $Poss(\alpha) = 1$, if α is consistent. In this way, the necessity and possibility measures capture upper and lower bounds, respectively, on whether a formula is *true*. Key axioms of these measures include the following.

$$Nec(\alpha \wedge \beta) = Min(Nec(\alpha), Nec(\beta))$$

$$Nec(\alpha \vee \beta) \geq Min(Nec(\alpha), Nec(\beta))$$

$$Poss(\alpha \vee \beta) = Max(Poss(\alpha), Poss(\beta))$$

$$Poss(\alpha \wedge \beta) \leq Min(Poss(\alpha), Poss(\beta))$$

Note the similarity with those given for necessity and possibility measures earlier. As in Chapter 3, we are representing sets by propositions, and using $\wedge$ for $\cap$, and $\vee$ for $\cup$.

In order to use possibilistic logic, we harness theorem proving techniques. In [DP87], the resolution principle (which was introduced in Chapter 2) has been extended to reasoning with possibilistic logic. To simplify our exposition, we restrict discussion to precise propositions, and not vague or imprecise data, and we just discuss resolution for necessity measures. The possibilistic version of the resolution rule is the following.

$$\frac{Nec(\alpha \vee \beta) \geq i \ , \ Nec(\neg \beta \vee \gamma) \geq j}{Nec(\alpha \vee \gamma) \geq Min(i,j)}$$

So, if i is the lower bound of the necessity of $\alpha \vee \beta$, and j is the lower bound of necessity of $\neg \alpha \vee \gamma$, then $Min(i,j)$ is the lower bound of the necessity of the resolvant $\alpha \vee \gamma$.

For a more comprehensive introduction to possibilistic logic, see [DP88a, KGK94, DLP94].

4.3.3 Using possibility theory

Possibility has been applied to reasoning with vague statements [Zad79, DP88b]. For example, suppose we have the following statement.

If the clothes are dirty then wash them in hot water

Both the concepts dirty and hot are vague or fuzzy in this context. We have already considered a membership function for hot water in Figure 4.2. For ascertaining the dirtiness of the clothes, we could soak the clothes in water for a few minutes, then drain the water off, and finally measure the opaqueness of the water. We could then give a membership function for dirty in terms of the opaqueness of the water. In order to provide a reference, or context, for these fuzzy sets, we assume a reference set. This is the set of values the concept could potentially take. For the hot water, we could choose the set of natural numbers from 0 to 150, representing 0C to 150C.

For the opaqueness, we could choose the natural numbers from 0 to 100, representing the percentage of opaqueness.

For a given collection of clothes, we are interested in using this general statement to determine whether to wash them in hot water. In other words, we wish to determine whether for some fuzzy value for dirty, we should derive the instruction to wash the clothes in hot water.

In classical logic *modus ponens* (an alternative name for implies elimination) is based on the argument that if α is *true* and $\alpha \rightarrow \beta$ is *true*, then β is *true*. For reasoning with fuzzy statements such as the one above about dirty clothes, we need to develop the notion of *modus ponens*. Generalized modus ponens is such a development [MS75].

For example, suppose the clothes are "not very dirty", then "not very dirty" does not directly match with "dirty". We need to adapt the statement to allow the data "not very dirty" to apply. This means changing the consequence in some way, perhaps to "warm water". Since, "dirty clothes" and "hot water" can be modelled by fuzzy sets, the manipulations can be done on the fuzzy sets. For this, we represent propositions as follows.

$$X \text{ is } A$$

So for example, "clothes are dirty" is a a proposition, where X is "clothes", and A is "dirty". Generalized modus ponens is then of the following form.

$$\frac{X \text{ is } A^* \qquad \text{If } X \text{ is } A, \text{ then } Y \text{ is } B}{Y \text{ is } B^*}$$

Here, B^* is calculated from the possibility distribution of A^*, and of A given B. The possibility distribution for B provides an upper bound on the possibility distribution for B^*. This calculation decreases the possibility that Y is B^* is *true*, the further A^* is from A.

4.4 Outlook for using fuzzy information

Fuzzy set theory constitutes a useful and intuitive extension of classical set theory for representing and reasoning with fuzzy information. However, as mentioned in Section 3.4, there is a lively debate on the relative merits of various approaches to uncertainty. This has included discussion over the necessity for the formalisms presented in this chapter — see for example [Che86, Zad86, Lin87, Fuz94a].

There are many applications where fuzzy information occurs. These range from fuzzy control systems for machines [Mam76, HO82] to fuzzy expert systems [Zad83]. For further information on the theory of fuzzy sets and systems, and on a variety of applications, see [DPY95, Fuz93, Fuz94b].

In this book we discuss applications in fuzzy rule-based systems (Chapter 7), fuzzy databases (Chapter 8), and information retrieval and information filtering (Chapter 9).

Chapter 5

Default Information

5.1 Introduction

It is noteworthy that people rely much more on exploiting general rules (not to be understood as universal laws), or defaults, than on a myriad of individual facts. Defaults tend to be less than 100% accurate, and so have exceptions. Nevertheless it is intuitive and advantageous to resort to defaults and therefore allow the inference of useful conclusions, even if it does entail making some mistakes, as not all exceptions to these defaults are necessarily known. Furthermore, it is often necessary to use defaults when we do not have sufficient information to allow us to specify or use universal laws.

Using default information requires non-monotonic reasoning. Interest in non-monotonic reasoning started with attempts to handle defaults of the form "if α holds, then β normally holds", where α and β are propositions. It is called non-monotonic because, as more information is acquired, an exception might arise, and hence the inference would have to be withdrawn. This contrasts with monotonic reasoning where if an inference is drawn from some database, that inference remains whatever further data is added to the database. Hence, non-monotonic reasoning allows for inferences to change if new information suggests it should, whereas monotonic reasoning is committed to its original inferences.

In the following subsection, we consider non-monotonic reasoning in more detail, and then consider some of the issues in formalizing it. In Section 5.2, we consider using default information in more detail, and present a formal method for handling it. In Section 5.3, we consider the outlook for using default information.

65

5.1.1 Non-monotonic reasoning is diverse

Non-monotonic reasoning is important in dialogue, in storing information, in learning, as a rule of conjecture, in the related issue of facilitating logical probability, and many other aspects of cognition.

Dialogue In dialogue many operations that could be described as conventions are used, with all participants normally accepting these conventions. During the course of a conversation many assumptions are made; so for example if exceptions are not made explicit, it is assumed, by default, the exceptions do not hold. The following example from McCarthy [McC86] illustrates this.

> "Suppose A tells B about a situation involving a bird. If the bird cannot fly, and this is relevant, then A must say so. Whereas if the bird can fly, there is no requirement to mention the fact. So, if I hire you to build me a bird cage and you don't put a top on it, I can get out of paying for it even if you tell the judge that I never said my bird could fly. However, if I complain that you wasted money by putting a top on a cage I intended for a penguin, the judge will agree with you that if the bird couldn't fly I should have said so."

Such conventions in dialogues are important in natural language understanding. They also have significant implications for engineering intelligent systems, in particular natural language interfaces and user modelling techniques. However, such considerations may extend beyond man-machine interfaces. Using the term "agent" to cover man and machine, then non-monotonicity will be required for more efficient and sophisticated agent-to-agent interaction.

Memory In storing information, non-monotonic reasoning can be used to adapt economy principles. For example, economies can be achieved by stating that whatever is not found to be true in a set of data is assumed to be false.

Conjecture As a rule of conjecture, if we have knowledge of the form "most As are Bs", then it is reasonable to use non-monotonic reasoning to make the conjecture that any given A is also a B. For example, most swans are white, and therefore for any given swan, I can make the default conjecture that it is a white swan.

Similarly, reasoning with defaults is an aspect of non-monotonic reasoning. For example, by default we assume that if we go to a shop on a weekday at 10am that it will be open. It is obvious that efficient, intelligent, reasoning would be impossible without recourse to such a default reasoning capability.

In some respects there is a probabilistic aspect to such defaults. However, the axioms of probability are not always appropriate for reasoning with such information. In particular, non-monotonic reasoning works in situations where insufficient conditional probabilities are known to allow probabilistic reasoning.

Learning Non-monotonic reasoning is also important in learning. In inductive learning, general rules are derived from data. When exceptions to those general rules are found, it is undesirable to reject those general rules, and learn new rules from scratch, since it is expensive and unnecessary. A non-monotonic approach means that exceptions can be handled without necessarily rejecting the general rules entirely.

In all these aspects of cognition, it is clear that the issue of "efficiency" is central to the role of non-monotonic reasoning. However, non-monotonic reasoning involves a degree of uncertainty. Default (or synonymously defeasible) assumptions are not always valid, because of exceptions. Therefore, efficiency comes at the price of some risk. This is well summarized by the following excerpts from Shoham [Sho88].

> "The general problem is how to reason efficiently about what is true over extended periods of time, and it has to do with certain trade-offs between risk-avoidance and economy in the process of prediction."

> "To summarize, it is the problem of trading off the amount of knowledge that is required in order to make inferences on the one hand, and the accuracy of those inferences on the other hand. In the particular context of predicting the future, it is the problem of making sound predictions about the future without taking into account everything about the past."

Indeed some of the key early arguments for research into non-monotonic reasoning were motivated by problems that confronted the compromise between "accurate" decision-making, and "efficient" decision-making. Key problems include the following:

Qualification problem: When making a decision, we usually do not check every relevant aspect prior to making the decision. Similarly, we do not check that every aspect of a plan is realizable before executing it. For example, if we are going to drive home in the evening from work, there are many relevant factors we could check such as checking that the engine is working properly, checking that the car still has four wheels, and phoning the traffic authorities to confirm the roads are not closed. Obviously, we do not make all these checks. We just jump into the car and go. Therefore, it can be viewed as the problem of restricting reasoning to only the information that is directly relevant. Hence, for formalizing non-monotonic reasoning, it involves problems of ascertaining what to check, without explicitly stating every conceivable exception for every possible situation.

Ramification problem: When reasoning about, for example, a plan, if we consider undertaking some action, then there are many possible ramifications. Yet it is likely that only a small proportion will be of significance. So the ramification problem is one of restricting consideration of the ramifications of actions to those that are directly relevant. For example, if we want to boil an egg, and we are in a state where the pan, with water and egg, is on the cooker, then when we execute the action of switching on the cooker, we still expect the pan, with water and egg, to have remained on the cooker. However, not all things remain constant. When moving from one state to another. For example, if I move the pan, then the water and egg also move. In reasoning about plans, when we undertake an action, if we have to specify whether every item in a state remains constant in the next state then it is not a very efficient mode of reasoning. So the ramification problem is one of ascertaining the important items that do change, and the important items that do not change, for any given action, without explicitly listing them all. This is also called the frame problem.

The qualification and ramification problems were first raised in the Naive Physics Manifesto [MH69]. This manifesto was part of a framework for modelling diverse physical phenomena in artificial intelligence, and it invoked a lot of work in non-monotonic reasoning.

5.1.2   Formalizing the use of default information

Non-monotonicity is an important feature of reasoning systems for intelligent systems. However, formalizing this kind of reasoning, hence facilitating the use of default information, is not always straightforward.

In this text, we use the terms non-monotonic reasoning, defeasible reasoning, and default reasoning as synonyms. We also use the terms non-monotonic logic and defeasible logic as synonyms, and we use the terms defeasible information and default information as synonyms. We reserve the term default logic for a particular formalism developed by Reiter [Rei80].

Non-monotonic reasoning involves the manipulation of two kinds of information, namely defeasible and non-defeasible. Non-defeasible information is always conclusive. For example, in classical logic information is non-defeasible. It is the information that is not going to be retracted, such as definitions. In applications, non-defeasible information may include mathematical rules, scientific laws (at least those that are regarded as beyond refutation), and geographical facts. In contrast, defeasible information is only justified when there is no reason not to believe it. Consider the following.

A match lights if struck

A match doesn't light if the match is wet

Such statements constitute "general" or default knowledge. However representing this kind of knowledge is not straightforward in classical logic. If for example the following assertions are represented in the knowledge-base with the defeasible information above, we do not want to infer a contradiction, since that would trivialize our reasoning. It is trivialized because any inference can be derived from an inconsistent database when using classical logic. We explain the problem of reasoning with inconsistent information further in Chapter 6. Returning to the above example, consider the following further facts.

A match is struck

A match is wet

To address this we need some mechanism to allow non-trivial reasoning. But furthermore, it should incorporate intuitive principles for identifying the more appropriate inferences. For example, in a database comprising the four statements above, it would be desirable to use a "principle of specificity" to derive the conclusion that the match doesn't light in preference to the conclusion that it does light.

As a first candidate for using default information, we may consider classical logic. Unfortunately, as we see from the above example, classical logic is unsatisfactory because it can be trivialized. Furthermore, there is a need, sometimes, to change conclusions in the light of new data added to the database. This facility to change conclusions is problematical for classical logic because it is monotonic. We define monotonicity below, where Δ is a set of classical formulae, α and β are classical formulae, and $\vdash$ denotes classical inference.

$$\frac{\Delta \vdash \alpha}{\Delta \cup \{\beta\} \vdash \alpha}$$

This means that if α is an inference from Δ, then α is still an inference after β is added to Δ. These shortcomings of classical logic therefore lead us to consider non-classical logics for our formalisms.

5.2   Default reasoning

There are many situations where default reasoning can enhance an information system. An application where it would be reasonable to use general rules would be for marketing, since many marketing decisions do not rely on 100% accurate information on every customer, but rather are based on generalities about customers. We use this as an example, in the next section, to introduce the nature and some of the advantages of default reasoning.

5.2.1   An application of default reasoning

In general, a person who is a customer of a telephone company has a telephone. Of course, exceptions do exist: deaf people for instance, have special machines that are not 'telephones' *stricto sensu*. So, if *jose-fernandez* is a customer of a telephone company then it makes sense to conclude that he has a telephone. The statement "a customer of a telephone company has a telephone, unless proven otherwise" is default information. The principle by which it occurs in reasoning is: "if X is a customer of a telephone company then X has a telephone, unless it is proven that X counts as an exception". We can represent this default information in the following form.

70

$$\frac{phone\text{-}customer(X) \ : \ \neg exception(X)}{has\text{-}phone(X)}.$$

Such a rule is applied as follows. Given a certain value, say *jose-fernandez*, for X, if

$$phone\text{-}customer(jose\text{-}fernandez)$$

is deduced and

$$exception(jose\text{-}fernandez)$$

cannot be proven, then the following is concluded, and it is called a default conclusion or default inference.

$$has\text{-}phone(jose\text{-}fernandez)$$

Notice that the principle governing the use of default information is extremely flexible: From the fact that *jose-fernandez* is a customer of a telephone company, and in the absence of any evidence as to the possibility that *jose-fernandez* counts as an exception, the general rule leads to the conclusion that *jose-fernandez* has a telephone. Importantly, there is no need to *prove* that *jose-fernandez* is not an exception (for instance, that he is not deaf). It is sufficient to establish that no proof is available according to which *jose-fernandez* would be some kind of an exception: Clearly this is much less demanding.

Furthermore, there is no need to have a list of all exceptions. For example, the following default information need not be modified as information about exceptions evolves.

$$\frac{phone\text{-}customer(X) \ : \ \neg exception(X)}{has\text{-}phone(X)}$$

Now, suppose that "deaf people have no phones", then adding the formula

$$\forall \ X \ deaf(X) \ \rightarrow \ exception(X)$$

is enough to block the default conclusion $has\text{-}phone(X)$ for an X that corresponds to a deaf person (while still permitting the default conclusion $has\text{-}phone(X)$ for an X that does not correspond to a deaf person). As an illustration, consider the following facts and default information.

71

$$phone\text{-}customer(ann\text{-}baker)$$

$$phone\text{-}customer(andy\text{-}cook)$$

$$deaf(andy\text{-}cook)$$

$$\frac{phone\text{-}customer(X) \; : \; \neg exception(X)}{has\text{-}phone(X)}$$

The above default rule can be applied to X being *ann-baker* because *phone-customer(ann-baker)* can be deduced and *exception(ann-baker)* cannot be proven, so the following default conclusion is inferred.

$$has\text{-}phone(ann\text{-}baker)$$

Now consider the case where X is *andy-cook*, and try to apply the default information.

$$\frac{phone\text{-}customer(X) \; : \; \neg exception(X)}{has\text{-}phone(X)}$$

Clearly, *phone-customer(andy-cook)* can be deduced. However, the general rule cannot be applied because *exception(andy-cook)* can be proven via the following formulae.

$$deaf(andy\text{-}cook)$$

$$\forall X \; deaf(X) \rightarrow \; exception(X)$$

Conveniently, any new exception discovered with time can be taken into account by simply adding them to the knowledge. Furthermore, there is no need to modify the general rule, which continues to stand as before, though, the general rule will cease to yield some previous conclusions (the ones corresponding to the newly found exceptions).

Here is an example. When only *phone-customer(jose-fernandez)* is known, the following is inferred.

$$has\text{-}phone(jose\text{-}fernandez)$$

If, in addition, the following are also known, then *has-phone(jose-fernandez)* is no longer inferred.

$$deaf(jose\text{-}fernandez)$$

$$\forall X \; deaf(X) \rightarrow \; exception(X)$$

Such a behaviour captures non-monotonic reasoning because a conclusion drawn in the presence of certain information is withdrawn on the introduction of additional specific information. That is, the set of conclusions does not increase monotonically as information increases.

An interesting observation is that some exceptions just fail to obey the general rule while others explicitly oppose it. For instance, for deaf people we might want to assert both of the following items of information.

$$\forall X \; deaf(X) \rightarrow \; exception(X)$$

$$\forall X \; deaf(X) \rightarrow \; \neg has\text{-}phone(X)$$

Whereas for hearing-impaired people, that also count as exceptions, we may merely want to stay agnostic about whether or not they have a phone, and assert only the following.

$$\forall X \; hearing\text{-}impaired(X) \rightarrow \; exception(X)$$

Also, there is no need to know the reason why an item is an exception to the general rule. Indeed, the following are sufficient to block the default conclusion, without providing a reason as to why *andy-baker* is a telephone customer who does not have a telephone.

$$phone\text{-}customer(andy\text{-}baker)$$

$$exception(andy\text{-}baker)$$

Observe that priorities between general rules can be rendered. Consider an example of a computer club whose members are using lines of the telephone equipped with modems to transmit data. They must count as exceptions to our general law, unless they have more than a single telephone line.

$$\frac{member\text{-}computer\text{-}club(X) \; : \; single\text{-}lined(X)}{exception(X)}.$$

Consider an individual *john-smith* such that the following facts hold.

$$phone\text{-}customer(john\text{-}smith)$$

$$member\text{-}computer\text{-}club(john\text{-}smith)$$

Because the fact $\neg single\text{-}lined(john\text{-}smith)$ cannot be proven, the inference $exception(john\text{-}smith)$ is obtained by this new rule, and the other earlier rule is blocked, i.e., $has\text{-}phone(john\text{-}smith)$ is not inferred. Indeed, if we try to apply the earlier rule first

$$\frac{phone\text{-}customer(X)\ :\ \neg exception(X)}{has\text{-}phone(X)}.$$

then $has\text{-}phone(john\text{-}smith)$ is inferred on the condition that the formula $\neg exception(john\text{-}smith)$ cannot be inferred. Applying the new rule now yields $exception(john\text{-}smith)$, violating the proviso imposed on the earlier application, and thus voiding it.

5.2.2   Default logic

Default logic by Reiter [Rei80] aims at formalizing reasoning from default information, by means of formulae of classical logic and the so-called default rules, namely the expressions of the following form, where α, β, γ are formulas of classical logic.

$$\frac{\alpha\ :\ \beta}{\gamma}$$

The inference rules are those of classical logic plus a special mechanism to deal with default rules: basically, if α is deduced and $\neg\beta$ cannot be inferred then infer γ, in which case β is possible.

We assume the usual set of classical logic formulae, which we denote as F. We let D denote the set of default rules. A database Δ is a subset of D $\cup$ F. An example of such a database is as follows.

$$\frac{phone\text{-}customer(andy\text{-}baker)\ :\ \neg exception(andy\text{-}baker)}{has\text{-}phone(andy\text{-}baker)}$$

$$\frac{phone\text{-}customer(ann\text{-}cook)\ :\ \neg exception(ann\text{-}cook)}{has\text{-}phone(ann\text{-}cook)}$$

$$phone\text{-}customer(andy\text{-}baker)$$

$$phone\text{-}customer(ann\text{-}cook)$$

In the following we provide the actual definition of an extension, which is a consistent set of conclusions of a database Δ. First, we introduce a function Γ that indicates what conclusions are to be associated with a given set of formulae. $\Gamma(E)$ is the smallest set of classical formulae such that the following three conditions hold:

All the classical formulae in Δ are in E.

All the classical formulae classically implied by E are in E.

For each default rule of the following form, if α is in $\Gamma(E)$ and $\neg\beta$ is not in E, then γ is in $\Gamma(E)$.

$$\frac{\alpha \;:\; \beta}{\gamma}$$

From this, E is an extension of Δ if and only if $E = \Gamma(E)$.

So for the above example, we have the following extension.

$$phone\text{-}customer(ann\text{-}cook)$$

$$phone\text{-}customer(andy\text{-}baker)$$

$$has\text{-}phone(ann\text{-}cook)$$

$$has\text{-}phone(andy\text{-}baker)$$

Further details on default logic, and variants of default logic, can be found in [Bes89, Bre91, MT93, GHR94].

5.2.3 Resolving conflicting arguments

It is perhaps now evident that using default, or defeasible information, and using inconsistent information are two inter-related problems. A significant part of reasoning with default rules is resolving inconsistencies. Similarly, many problems of inconsistencies in information arise from the use of default information.

In reasoning with both inconsistent information and default information, there is the question of whether to adopt a skeptical or credulous view. In a skeptical view, the logic is cautious and does not allow conflicting inferences, whereas in a credulous view, the logic is less cautious, and does allow conflicting inferences. The rationale behind a credulous view is that the user makes a selection from the conflicting inferences. For example, take the following defaults,

$$\frac{aircraft(X) : require\text{-}runway(X)}{require\text{-}runway(X)}$$

$$\frac{helicopter(X) : \neg require\text{-}runway(X)}{\neg require\text{-}runway(X)}$$

and the following facts.

$$aircraft(sikorsky)$$

$$helicopter(sikorsky)$$

From this, there are two extensions, one with $require\text{-}runway(sikorsky)$ and the other with $\neg require\text{-}runway(sikorsky)$. A credulous view would allow both $require\text{-}runway(sikorsky)$ and $\neg require\text{-}runway(sikorsky)$ as possible inferences, whereas a skeptical view would allow neither. However, it is not clear in general when reasoning should be skeptical or credulous.

One solution to these kinds of problem is to label the default rules, and then use the labels to resolve the conflict. Essentially, the labels can be used to capture extra information about the formulae in the database, and about the inferences, so that a judicious choice can be made. For a variety of applications labelling meets the need for extra information about data [Gab93, Gab96]. This may be further object-level information, or meta-level information, or semantic information.

A label can represent a wide variety of notions. Take the labelled formula k: α. The label k could capture any of the following for example:

- the fuzzy reliability of α

- the origin, or source, of α

- the priority of α

- the time when α holds

- the proof of α

76

So for example, with the database about aircraft, we could introduce an ordering over labelled formulae that captures a notion of specificity. For the above database, the default,

$$\frac{helicopter(X) : \neg require\text{-}runway(X)}{\neg require\text{-}runway(X)}$$

is more specific than the default,

$$\frac{aircraft(X) : require\text{-}runway(X)}{require\text{-}runway(X)}$$

since helicopters are a sub-class of aircraft. The ordering can then be used to allow the inference $\neg require\text{-}runway(sikorsky)$ to be derived in preference to its complement. The justification in this case would be that the rule about helicopters is for use with exceptions, namely helicopters, to the rule about aircraft, and is therefore preferable for reasoning in the context of helicopters. Analyses of reasoning with priorities include [Bre89, Bre91, Bre94, CHS93]. See also Section 6.5.2.

5.2.4   Implementation of inference engine

There are experimental implementations of automated reasoning systems for default logic and related logics [JK90, NR92, Nie94, Hop93, Sch95, RS94, LS95]. These include systems that compute extensions and systems that provide credulous and skeptical query-answering.

An inference engine can be viewed as being composed of classical reasoning and conflict resolution. For classical reasoning, promising automated reasoning techniques exist. Both classical deduction and consistency checking can be used in default reasoning. Conflict resolution presents the new computational challenge in default reasoning. The initial search space for the conflict resolution task is exponential with respect to the number of default rules and brute force search methods are able to handle only very modest sized sets of default rules.

For certain classes of default databases, where the interaction of default rules is limited, there exist techniques to solve the conflict resolution task in polynomial time [NR92]. However, to further improve conflict resolution, there is a need to focus on: (i) developing techniques for exploiting relevancy, by answering a query using only the relevant part of the default database; (ii) pruning of the search space for conflict resolution [Nie94, Sch95], and (iii) approximation of default reasoning [BS94].

77

5.3   Outlook for using default information

The notion of defaults covers a diverse variety of information, including heuristics, rules of conjecture, null values in databases, closed world assumptions for databases, and some qualitative abstractions of probabilistic information. Defaults are a natural and very common form of information. There are also obvious advantages to applying the same default a number of times. There is an economy in stating (and dealing with) only a general proposition instead of stating (and dealing with) maybe thousands of instances of such a general proposition. Furthermore, using default knowledge is complementary to using statistical knowledge. For more information on default information and non-monotonic reasoning see [Gin87, GHR94].

Current technology for using default knowledge (such as knowledge-based systems shells) is predominantly implementation-dependent and/or *ad hoc* (such as daemons, default values, and inheritance). This causes problems for development and maintenance. We can address this by adopting the formal approach of default logics.

The industrial relevance of using default knowledge is now being elucidated. In the short term, there are a series of promising applications in information systems. In particular in enhancing information retrieval (e.g. online databases), information filtering (e.g. online news services and email systems), merging information (e.g. from heterogeneous databases), and information routing (e.g. in email and groupware systems). In each of these applications, there is uncertainty about the contents of the information, and about the best way of handling (such as filtering, retrieving, merging, or routing) that information. Default knowledge can be used to address this uncertainty by capturing rules about the semantic relationships between information, and of heuristics for handling information. We consider this topic in more detail in Chapter 9.

Similarly, in order to limit the size of databases, there is a need for default information, such as general rules that are usually true, though accepted to have some exceptions. For example, a market research agency will profitably resort to consumer profiles that are not 100% accurate, and hence, a database of such consumer profiles will include default information. We consider this in more detail in Chapter 8.

Chapter 6

Inconsistent Information

6.1 Introduction

Intellectual activities usually involve reasoning with different perspectives. For example, consider negotiation, learning, or merging multiple opinions. Central to reasoning with different perspectives is the issue of handling inconsistencies. Maintaining absolute consistency is not always possible. Often it is not even desirable since this can unnecessarily constrain the intellectual activity, and can lead to the loss of important information. Indeed, since the real-world forces us to work with inconsistencies, we should formalize some of the usually informal or extra-logical ways of responding to them. This is not necessarily done by eradicating inconsistencies, but rather by supplying logical rules specifying how we should act on them [GH91, GH93a]. In this way, we are moving away from a classical view of information being either true or false, to a view where we accept that we may have a number of perspectives on information and that these perspectives may contradict each other.

To illustrate this approach consider an airline booking system. It is normal practice for an airline to sell more tickets for a flight than there are seats on the flight. Even though this situation is inconsistent with the safety regulations, the airline will maintain the inconsistency until shortly before departure. The airline supports the inconsistency because it expects that not enough passengers will actually show up at the airport, and therefore that the inconsistency will resolve itself. Furthermore, by maintaining the "overbooking inconsistency" the airline can make more money. This is therefore an example of there being a cost-benefit in maintaining an inconsistency, and indeed of the inconsistency being desirable for the airline.

However, supporting this kind of inconsistency sometimes leads to difficult situations when, prior to departure, more people have checked in than expected. In this eventuality the airline staff are required to take some kind of action such as upgrading tourist class passengers to business class, or offering free tickets to passengers who are prepared to catch a later flight. In extreme situations they may even provide an extra aircraft. But despite the expense of some of these actions, they are rarely invoked, and therefore the "overbooking inconsistency" is cost-effective overall. Furthermore, we are so used to the wider context of the airline inconsistency that some people might not even recognize it as an inconsistency.

Inconsistency handling in the booking system is an example of a general phenomenon found in database applications. Viewing the environment containing such databases, and the circumstances surrounding each inconsistency, indicates that we need to consider inconsistencies in terms of how and why they arise, and the actions that are performed on them. Indeed describing an inconsistency via the wider context of the database allows us to move away from the negative view of an inconsistency within a database.

There are many other cases of database systems that can be described in a similar way to the booking system. For example, in a government tax database, inconsistencies in a taxpayer's records are used to invoke inquiries into that taxpayer. Indeed from the perspective of the tax inspector, this is another application where inconsistencies are useful and desirable [BdCGH95].

Another important example is in systems development. The development of most large and complex systems necessarily involves many people, each with their own perspectives on the system. Systems development therefore involves problems of identifying and handling inconsistencies between such perspectives. For this there is a need to tolerate inconsistencies, and more importantly to be able to act in a context-dependent way in response to inconsistency [FGH+94]. This is vital since inflexible forcing of consistency can unnecessarily constrain the development process.

There are many situations in which some information and its contrary appear. In some situations it is useful such as in the tax collection database, since it can initiate profitable enquiries. In other situations it is undesirable, such as in a bank database on customer accounts, where the inconsistency needs to be located and the database revised.

In some situations it is not even clear that an inconsistency can be acted upon or the database revised. For example, the tax agency database may include items of legislation such as each citizen can only have one spouse. Now, suppose, quite unexpectedly from the point of view of the database designer, that the tax agency database has a taxpayer who has two spouses. This causes an inconsistency. Furthermore, it might not be the most appropriate solution to revise the form of the database.

$$\forall X, Y, Z \; spouse(X,Y) \land spouse(X,Z) \rightarrow Y = Z$$

$$spouse(mr\text{-}bigamist, ms\text{-}victim)$$

$$spouse(mr\text{-}bigamist, ms\text{-}misled)$$

$$ms\text{-}victim \neq ms\text{-}misled$$

Once we allow uncertainty of any kind into our information system, we must also incorporate a reasoning component to derive answers from the more general information in the database. To design that component, we need to build on an appropriate formal model of deduction. As a first candidate we may consider classical logic. Unfortunately, classical logic is unsatisfactory because it allows any conclusion to be drawn from inconsistent information in a database. This is because the classical logic incorporates the following proof rule, called *ex falso quodlibet* (or negate elimination).

$$\frac{\alpha, \quad \neg\alpha}{\beta}$$

This proof rule reads that from the two items α and $\neg\alpha$, conclude β. Applying it to *mr-bigamist*'s case does not look good. We could apply *ex falso quodlibet* to draw quite irrelevant and inappropriate conclusions such as the following.

$$rain\text{-}falls(mainly\text{-}on\text{-}the\text{-}plain)$$

What we really require for reasoning with such databases is a logic that does not support such trivialization. Solutions to the problem of inconsistent data include database revision and paraconsistent logics. The first approach effectively removes data from the database to produce a new consistent database. In contrast, the second approach leaves the database inconsistent, but prohibits the logics from deriving trivial inferences. Unfortunately, the first approach means we may lose useful information since we may be forced to make a premature selection of our new database, or we

81

may not even be able to make a selection. We consider here the advantages and disadvantages of the paraconsistent approach.

The primary objective of this chapter is to present a range of paraconsistent logics that give sensible inferences from inconsistent information. We consider (1) Weakly-negative logics which use a subset of the classical proof rules; (2) Four-valued logic which uses an intuitive four-valued semantics; and (3) Quasi-classical logic which gives classical reasoning without trivialization by restricting the use of the classical proof rules.

These options behave in quite different ways with data. None can be regarded as perfect for handling inconsistent information in general. Rather, they provide a spectrum of approaches. However, in all the approaches we cover, we aim to stay close to classical reasoning, since classical logic has many appealing features for knowledge representation and reasoning.

6.2 Weakly-negative logics

To avoid trivialization, weakly-negative logics compromise the classical proof theory. These logics use the same language as classical logic, but use a subset of the proof rules. This means that for any given database we may get fewer conclusions. They allow, for example, normal notions of conjunction, such as $\alpha \wedge \beta$ gives α, but they are substantially weaker in terms of negation. There are a number of ways in which this weakening can be achieved. One way is to weaken classical logic so that *ex falso quodlibet* does not hold. This gives a paraconsistent logic called C_ω logic proposed by da Costa [dC74].

The C_ω logic is usually presented as a set of axiom schema. This is a common form of presentation for logics. Each schema can be instantiated with formulae, and then used as a new formula. Essentially, a schema is a "mould" for composing formulae. Reasoning is by application of implies elimination (as discussed in Chapter 2). So for example, suppose the following is an axiom schema.

$$\alpha \wedge \beta \rightarrow \alpha$$

We can instantiate this with $\phi \vee \psi$ for α, and ρ for β, to give the following.

$$(\phi \vee \psi) \wedge \rho \rightarrow (\phi \vee \psi)$$

Suppose we also have the data $(\phi \vee \psi) \wedge \rho$, then we can derive $\phi \vee \psi$ using implies elimination.

The logic C_ω is defined by the following axiom schema. All these schema are also schema in classical logic.

$$\alpha \to (\beta \to \alpha)$$
$$(\alpha \to \beta) \to ((\alpha \to (\beta \to \gamma)) \to (\alpha \to \gamma))$$
$$\alpha \wedge \beta \to \alpha$$
$$\alpha \wedge \beta \to \beta$$
$$\alpha \to (\beta \to \alpha \wedge \beta)$$
$$\alpha \to \alpha \vee \beta$$
$$\beta \to \alpha \vee \beta$$
$$(\alpha \to \gamma) \to ((\beta \to \gamma) \to (\alpha \vee \beta \to \gamma))$$
$$\alpha \vee \neg\alpha$$
$$\neg\neg\alpha \to \alpha$$

To illustrate the use of C_ω, consider the following example. In this example, there is a symmetry about whether or not α is a δ. In other words, there is an argument that α is a δ, and an argument that α is $\neg\delta$.

$$\alpha \to (\beta \wedge \gamma)$$
$$\gamma \to \delta$$
$$\beta \to \neg\delta$$
$$\alpha$$

Using the proof theory we can derive inferences including α, β and γ. We can also derive both δ and $\neg\delta$.

Reasoning that is supported by C_ω also includes using quantifiers. So for example, for the following data.

$$\forall X, Y \ spouse(X, Y) \to spouse(Y, X)$$

$$spouse(mr\text{-}martin, mrs\text{-}martin)$$

we can infer the following.

$$spouse(mrs\text{-}martin, mr\text{-}martin)$$

Following from the axiom schema, reasoning that is supported by C_ω includes the rule of disjunctive introduction.

$$\frac{\alpha \to \gamma, \quad \beta \to \gamma}{\alpha \vee \beta \to \gamma}$$

In many ways, C_ω is a useful substitute for classical logic. But it does lack some intuitive proof rules, such as *modus tollens*.

$$\frac{\alpha \to \beta \, , \ \neg\beta}{\neg\alpha}$$

So for example, for the following data,

$$\forall X, Y \ spouse(X, Y) \to spouse(Y, X)$$

$$\neg spouse(mr\text{-}martin, mrs\text{-}jones)$$

the following conclusion cannot be derived, even though it is clearly a desirable inference.

$$\neg spouse(mrs\text{-}jones, mr\text{-}martin)$$

Resolution (or disjunctive syllogism) also fails.

$$\frac{\alpha \vee \beta, \neg\beta}{\alpha}$$

Furthermore, many useful equivalences fail such as the following, where $\equiv$ denotes equivalent, and $\not\equiv$ denotes not equivalent.

$$\neg\alpha \vee \beta \not\equiv \alpha \to \beta$$

$$\neg\neg\alpha \not\equiv \alpha$$

In this sense weakly-negative logics are sub-systems of classical logic. In particular compromising on negation means that many classical inference steps involving negation fail in weakly-negative logics. But to illustrate the sensitivity of this compromise, consider the following example. From the schema,

$$\alpha \to (\beta \to \alpha)$$

we can derive the following axiom.

$$\alpha \to (\neg\beta \to \alpha)$$

Now assume contraposition, a very natural form of classical reasoning, in the following form.

$$(\neg\beta \to \alpha) \to (\neg\alpha \to \beta)$$

By transitivity, which is a property that holds for C_ω, this would give

$$\alpha \to (\neg\alpha \to \beta)$$

which is a form of *ex falso quodlibet*. Hence, contraposition cannot be part of this compromise, and so is another example of classical reasoning that does not hold in C_ω.

Returning to our original data on *mr-bigamist*, a weakly-negative logic allows us to derive useful conclusions about the data. Furthermore, it is very robust in the sense that no matter what information is introduced into the database, the reasoning patterns will always give sensible conclusions in light of what has been introduced into the database.

Another advantage of a weakly-negative logic is that it does not force any decision to be made on whether any particular item of information is "false" in the database. So for example, we are not forced to decide whether the following is false.

$$spouse(mr\text{-}bigamist, ms\text{-}victim)$$

as opposed to the following.

$$spouse(mr\text{-}bigamist, ms\text{-}misled)$$

Similarly, we do not have to make a choice about which of *ms-misled* $\neq$ *ms-victim* and *ms-misled* = *ms-victim* hold.

The computational complexity of the deduction method presented is similar to classical logic. This is in contrast to the usual non-monotonic logics, where complexity is extremely high. This is due to the fact that paraconsistent logics block certain deductions from inconsistencies, whereas many non-monotonic logics, such as default logic, use consistency checking to ensure that each extension is free from inconsistencies.

The logic C_ω is only one of a number of interesting weakly-negative logics (for a review see [BdCGH95]). Weakly-negative logics are useful for rule-based reasoning with information since the logic supports implies elimination. They can be used to give guidance on the inconsistency and facilitate actions that should be taken on the database. Furthermore, they can be used without recourse to consistency checks. Finally, weakly-negative logics can be used as a formal basis for truth maintenance [MS88].

However, the removal of certain classical inference rules means that the propositional connectives in the language do not behave in a classical fashion. The interdefinability of the classical connectives has been traded in exchange for non-trivialization [Bes91]. This might be considered confusing and counter-intuitive for some users of information systems.

6.3 Four-valued logic

The four-valued logic of Belnap [Bel77] provides an interesting alternative to the weakly-negative logics in that it has an illuminating and intuitive semantic characterization to complement its proof theory. To simplify our exposition, we only consider the set of formulae composed using disjunction, conjunction and negation.

A formula in the language can be one of *true*, *false*, *both* or *neither*. For the database $\{\alpha, \neg\alpha, \beta\}$, α is *both*, $\neg\alpha$ is *both*, β is *true*, and γ is *neither*. This therefore provides a natural way of handling the problem of too much information.

We can view these truth values in terms of an "Approximation lattice" (see Figure 6.1). As more "information" is obtained about a formula, the truth-value "increases". In other words, if we know nothing about a formula, it is *neither*. Then as we gain some information it becomes either *true* or *false*. Finally, if we gain too much information it becomes *both*.

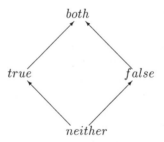

Figure 6.1: The "Approximation lattice"

For the semantics, we assume a distributive lattice, the "Logical lattice" (see Figure 6.2). Let P and Q each denote one of the truth values. If P is above Q in the logical lattice or P and Q are the same truth value, then $P \wedge Q$ has the truth value Q, and $P \vee Q$ has the truth value P.

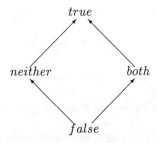

Figure 6.2: The "Logical lattice"

The truth tables, Table 6.1 – Table 6.3, for the negation, conjunction and disjunction connectives make explicit the use of the "Logical lattice".

α	*neither*	*false*	*true*	*both*
$\neg\alpha$	*neither*	*true*	*false*	*both*

Table 6.1: Truth table for negation

$\wedge$	*neither*	*false*	*true*	*both*
neither	*neither*	*false*	*neither*	*false*
false	*false*	*false*	*false*	*false*
true	*neither*	*false*	*true*	*both*
both	*false*	*false*	*both*	*both*

Table 6.2: Truth table for conjunction

$\vee$	*neither*	*false*	*true*	*both*
neither	*neither*	*neither*	*true*	*true*
false	*neither*	*false*	*true*	*both*
true	*true*	*true*	*true*	*true*
both	*true*	*both*	*true*	*both*

Table 6.3: Truth table for disjunction

To illustrate the use of four-valued logic, consider a situation where data is compiled from a number of sources. For example, consider the following data where each item has a truth value of either *true* or *both*.

$$employed(mr\text{-}jones)$$

$$\neg employed(mr\text{-}jones)$$

$$pay\text{-}tax(mr\text{-}jones)$$

$$\neg employed(mr\text{-}jones) \vee pay\text{-}tax(mr\text{-}jones)$$

In this example, suppose the first two items have the truth value *both*, whereas the third item has truth value *true*. For the fourth item, the sub-formula on the left of the disjunct is *both*, and the sub-formula on the right is *true*. Hence, by using the truth tables, we can ascertain that the formula is *true*.

There is no formula in the language of four-valued logic such that the semantics always gives the truth value *true*. However, there are formulae that never take the value *false*, such as for example $\alpha \vee \neg\alpha$.

Four-valued logic provides a natural and intuitive alternative to weakly-negative logics. The semantic characterization based on the approximation lattice (Figure 6.1) and logical lattice (Figure 6.2) could be applicable for reasoning with facts. However, there are problems with reasoning with formulae, particularly with respect to the lack of implies elimination and disjunctive syllogism. As with weakly-negative logics, the four-valued logic can be used without recourse to consistency checks.

6.4   Quasi-classical logic

As we have seen with weakly-negative logics and with four-valued logics, the weakening of the proof theory means that the connectives do not behave in a classical fashion. To address this, an alternative called quasi-classical logic (QC logic) has been proposed [BH95]. The proof theory is based on finding clauses that follow from the data by resolution, a proof rule that we introduced in Chapter 2. In order to make the proof theory applicable to any formula, we also require the notion of conjunctive normal form. Formulae are in conjunctive normal form if they are of the following form,

$$\alpha_1 \wedge .. \wedge \alpha_n$$

where each α_i is of the following form, and each β_m is an atomic proposition or the negation of an atomic proposition.

$$\beta_1 \vee .. \vee \beta_m$$

In general, a classical formula can appear complex: There may be many levels of nesting of the connectives. Representing a formula in conjunctive normal form removes this problem since there are at most two levels of nesting of the connectives. This then allows a straightforward application of resolution.

We now consider how to present a formula in conjunctive normal form. Apart from an atomic proposition, any formula is composed from smaller formulae. We call these smaller formula the subformulae of a formula. For any classical formula α, a conjunctive normal form of α can be produced by the application of distributivity, double negation elimination, and de Morgan rewrites on any subformulae, as defined in Table 6.4.

Double negation rewrite	$\neg\neg\alpha \Rightarrow \alpha$
De Morgan's rewrite	$\neg(\alpha \wedge \beta) \Rightarrow \neg\alpha \vee \neg\beta$ $\neg(\alpha \vee \beta) \Rightarrow \neg\alpha \wedge \neg\beta$
Distribution rewrite	$(\alpha \vee \beta) \wedge \gamma \Rightarrow (\alpha \wedge \gamma) \vee (\beta \wedge \gamma)$ $(\alpha \wedge \beta) \vee \gamma \Rightarrow (\alpha \vee \gamma) \wedge (\beta \vee \gamma)$
Implication rewrite	$\alpha \rightarrow \beta \Rightarrow \neg\alpha \vee \beta$

Table 6.4: Rewrites on subformulae to give conjunctive normal form

As an example, consider the following formula which we will rewrite into conjunctive normal form.

$$(\phi \vee \psi) \rightarrow \neg\neg\rho$$

First we can apply double negation rewrite to the subformula $\neg\neg\rho$ to give the following.

89

$$(\phi \lor \psi) \rightarrow \rho$$

Then we can apply implication rewrite to give the following.

$$\neg(\phi \lor \psi) \lor \rho$$

Now, we can apply de Morgan's rewrite to the subformula $\neg(\phi \land \psi)$ to give the following formula.

$$(\neg\phi \land \neg\psi) \lor \rho$$

Finally, we apply distribution rewrite to give the following, which is in conjunctive normal form.

$$(\neg\phi \lor \rho) \land (\neg\psi \lor \rho)$$

The proof theory of QC logic provides the power to derive a conjunctive normal form of any formula, together with the power of resolution. Only as a last step in any derivation is disjunct introduction allowed. This means that any resolvent of a set of formulae can be derived, but no trivial formulae can be derived. All the QC proof rules hold in classical logic, but the logic is weaker than classical logic in the way it is used.

To illustrate the use of QC in a software engineering setting, consider the following example. Suppose, we have two partial specifications VP1 and VP2. In VP1, there is the relation,

$$has\text{-}exactly\text{-}one(cashier, terminal)$$

and in VP2 there is the relation,

$$has\text{-}exactly\text{-}two(cashier, terminal)$$

In addition there is the following rule.

$$\forall X, Y \ has\text{-}exactly\text{-}one(X, Y) \leftrightarrow \neg has\text{-}exactly\text{-}two(X, Y)$$

This rule together with VP1 and VP2 is inconsistent. However, the definitions of the relations *has-exactly-one* and *has-exactly-two* also imply the following constraints.

$$\forall X, Y \ has\text{-}exactly\text{-}one(X, Y) \rightarrow has\text{-}one\text{-}or\text{-}more(X, Y)$$

$$\forall X, Y \ has\text{-}exactly\text{-}two(X, Y) \rightarrow has\text{-}one\text{-}or\text{-}more(X, Y)$$

Hence for both VP1 and VP2, and despite the inconsistency between them, we can derive the potentially useful non-trivial inference:

$$has\text{-}one\text{-}or\text{-}more(cashier, terminal)$$

Developing a non-trivializable, or paraconsistent, logic necessitates some compromise, or weakening, of classical logic. QC logic provides a means to obtain all the non-trivial resolvents from a set of formulae, without the problem of trivial clauses also following. Though the constraints on QC logic result in classical tautologies (formulae such as $\alpha \vee \neg\alpha$) not being derivable from the empty set, this is not usually a problem for applications.

QC logic exhibits the nice feature that no attention need to be paid to a special form that premises should have. This is in contrast with other paraconsistent logics, such as the weakly-negative logics, where two formulae identical by definition of a connective in classical logic may not yield the same set of conclusions.

QC logic is also more appropriate than various approaches to reasoning from consistent subsets of inconsistent sets of formulae (for a review see [BCD+93]). In particular, QC logic does not suffer from the limitation due to "breaking off" formulae into compatible pieces: QC logic can make use of the contents of the formulae without being constrained by a consistency check. Moreover, it is obviously an advantage of QC logic to dispense with the costly consistency checks that are needed in all approaches to reasoning from consistent subsets. Though this advantage also holds for weakly-negative logics and four-valued logic.

6.5 Handling inconsistent information

Paraconsistent logics allow useful conclusions from data: (1) They are robust, in the sense that the conclusions are not trivial with respect to the data; (2) There is no obligation to resolve the inconsistency, the logics behave satisfactorily irrespective of the inconsistency remaining; and (3) The logics can give guidance on the source of the inconsistency. Unfortunately paraconsistent logics only avoid the problems of trivialization that come with inconsistency. They don't offer strategies for acting on inconsistency. To address this, we consider, below, truth maintenance systems and resolving conflicting arguments.

91

6.5.1 Truth maintenance systems

A truth maintenance system records information about each inference that is generated from a set of assumptions. Two main approaches are justification-based truth maintenance [Doy79], which involves recording the proof for each inference, and assumption-based truth maintenance [Kle86], which involves recording the original assumptions used to produce each inference. When an inconsistency is identified, certain beliefs or assumptions are ignored. In this way, an inconsistency is isolated, and trivialization avoided.

6.5.2 Resolving conflicting arguments

So far in this chapter, we have restricted consideration to a classical language with no extra connectives or other notation. However, there have been a variety of interesting proposals for reasoning with inconsistent information that do extend the language. These include extending the language with labels and markers, priorities, default and defeasible connectives, and modal operators. We focus on labelling in this section.

In practical reasoning, object-level formulae can represent many kinds of useful information. However, it is possible to augment the syntactic information by semantic or meta-level information as proposed in labelled deductive systems [Gab93, Gab96]. The extra information contained in this kind of augmentation is then used by the logic to affect the outcome of the reasoning. We can represent the extra information for a formula α by some label i, and then represent this as $i : \alpha$, where the label is always juxtaposed to the formula. We discussed the application of this approach to default reasoning in Chapter 5. Indeed, it is perhaps now evident that using default information and using inconsistent information are two inter-related problems. A significant part of reasoning with default rules is resolving inconsistencies. Similarly, many problems of inconsistencies in information arise from the use of default information. So, for example, as with the default case, we can use labels to resolve problems of credulous and skeptical reasoning.

As another example of how labels can be used to resolve conflict, consider a work-group system that collates office memos on company regulations, and users query this system about these regulations. Suppose that information in memo {7} includes the following statement,

$$\{7\} : export\text{-}customer(X) \rightarrow charge\text{-}customer\text{-}in\text{-}dollars(X)$$

and memo {8} includes the following statements.

$$\{8\} : export\text{-}customer(X) \rightarrow charge\text{-}customer\text{-}in\text{-}deutchmarks(X)$$

$$\{8\} : \neg charge\text{-}customer\text{-}in\text{-}dollars(X)$$
$$\vee \neg charge\text{-}customer\text{-}in\text{-}deutchmarks(X)$$

If a user has the fact *export-customer(philips)* then the data is inconsistent. However, if the labels correspond to the data of the memo, then there is a preference for information from the more recent memo.

In this example, if $\{7\}$ corresponds to 23 January 1996, and $\{8\}$ corresponds to 25 February 1996, then the inconsistency can be resolved. As before, if new information is added to the system, such as new memos, then inferences might have to be retracted. This further illustrates the close relationship between reasoning with inconsistent information and reasoning with defeasible information.

Using labelling we generalize our notion of a database. If a formula $i : \alpha$ is in a database Δ, then we do not necessarily assume that α is "true". The meaning assigned to α is in part dependent on the label. So for example, i could mean that α was "true" yesterday, but not necessarily today, or i could mean that α is "true" if there is no formula $k : \beta$ such that k is more preferred to i. In this way, we actually only reason with the subset of our data that is actually "true".

Labelled languages, for example [GH93b], involve uniquely labelling the data, and amending the proof rules to propagate the labels: The consequent of each proof rule has a label that is a function of the labels of the premises. In this way, any inferences from the logic are labelled with information about the data and proof rules used to derive them. This means we can track information used in reasoning and hence analyse inconsistencies as they arise. We can identify likely sources of the problem, and use this to suggest appropriate actions.

There are other attempts to accommodate inconsistent data in a database by labelling. We can view ideas of truth maintenance in this way [Feh93]. Also, Balzer [Bal91] suggests "guards" on inconsistent data to minimize the negative ramifications, and then to warn the user of the inconsistency, and in Naqui and Rossi [NR90] inconsistent data is allowed to enter the database, but the time that the data is entered is recorded, and the newer data takes precedence over the older data when resolving inconsistencies.

Priorities have also been used in a number of ways in the management of inconsistency, and in the closely related problem of non-monotonic reasoning. This includes the use of specificity [Poo85], ordered theory presentations [Rya92], prioritized default logic [Bre94], and prioritized syntax-based entailment [BCD+93]. For more general issues of handling arguments, see [Lou87, Pra93, KAEGF95, EGH95].

6.6 Outlook for using inconsistent information

In practical reasoning, it is common to have "too much" information about some situation. In other words, it is common for there to be classically inconsistent information in a practical reasoning database [BdCGH95]. Yet intellectual activities usually involve reasoning with different perspectives. For example, consider negotiation, learning, or merging multiple opinions. Paraconsistent logics including weakly-negative, four-valued and quasi-classical logic offer a range of techniques for reasoning with inconsistent information.

This contrasts with many approaches which force consistency without consideration of the environment in which the data is used. Belief revision theory ensures consistency by rejecting formulae upon finding inconsistency [Gar88]. Similar proposals have been made for amending a database when finding inconsistency during updating (for example [FUV83]). Even more restrictive is the use of integrity constraints in databases, which prohibit inconsistent data even entering the database.

In this chapter, we have motivated the need to reason with inconsistent information, and to identify appropriate actions to respond to inconsistency. We have introduced some paraconsistent logics, and indicated ways that they can be used. Then we considered handling inconsistent information, in particular resolving conflicting arguments. We develop this theme by considering data fusion in Chapter 8, and on using inconsistent information in systems engineering in Chapter 10.

Chapter 7

Uncertainty in Knowledge-based Systems

7.1 Introduction

Knowledge-based systems are now used for a variety of commercial and professional tasks [And89]. Though, most of these are restricted to either using information that is certain or to using *ad hoc* techniques for handling uncertain information. This situation is likely to change as uncertainty techniques become better developed and as the need to harness more complex uncertain information becomes increasingly pressing.

Whilst some knowledge-based systems are stand-alone applications that use uncertainty techniques, others are vehicles for incorporating uncertainty handling into other kinds of information system, some of which we discuss in subsequent chapters.

In this chapter, we review three key approaches to developing knowledge-based systems, namely rule-based systems, case-based systems, and Bayesian network systems. For each, we review the basic features, making reference to the uncertainty approaches discussed in Chapters 3 to 6.

7.1.1 Decision-support systems

As the name implies, decision-support systems are computer programs that aid users in making decisions. They may be for supporting planning, diagnosis, scheduling, prediction, estimating, analysing rules or regulations, advising on procedures, or one of many other other kinds of decision-making tasks. They are often developed for clearly delineated domains, and may operate by modelling aspects of the reasoning, by presenting relevant information, or by undertaking calculations.

Whatever approach to decision-support systems is adopted, the choice of uncertainty methodology is complicated by the need of the decision-support system to explain its reasoning. So for example, a conclusion might be more readily accepted if the explanation is in some intuitive qualitative calculus rather than in some complex statistical form.

Uncertainty reasoning should also be considered in the wider context of the end user of the reasoning from the system. For example, the degree of reliance a user might put on the advice proffered by a system may have important ramifications in applications. If the user is involved in safety-critical decision making then there could be much risk involved in relying on the decision-support system. In this case, the user might have more confidence in the reasoning from the system if the knowledge is based on a comprehensive body of statisitical knowledge rather than some heuristics.

Therefore, the choice of uncertainty approach can be sensitive to a number of factors that may include the following.

- The type of information used.

- The quality of information used.

- The lucidity of the information used.

- The user's confidence in the information used.

- The lucidity of the reasoning system.

- The user's confidence in the reasoning system.

- The kinds of decision making.

- The reliance the user puts on the decision-support system.

- The ramifications of incorrect reasoning from the system.

In general, the choice of uncertainty approach is a compromise between a range of factors relevant to an application.

7.1.2 Embedded knowledge-based systems

Increasingly, knowledge-based systems are being embedded in larger information systems. Here, the knowledge-based system might act as a front-end to an information system, assisting the user in querying the information system. For example, knowledge-based systems can be used as intelligent front-ends to databases, as information retrieval tools, or as tools for navigating information repositories.

Alternatively, an embedded information system might be inside the information system and the user might be quite unaware of the existence of the knowledge-based system. For example, knowledge-based systems can be used to undertake integrity checking in databases, routing electronic documents in a work-group system, or acting as part of a security system in a network.

In the following chapters, we discuss embedded knowledge-based systems as tools for database systems (Chapter 8), and for information retrieval and information filtering in online information systems (Chapter 9).

7.2 Rule-based systems

In a rule-based system, rules act on facts to give conclusions. Uncertainty may be associated with both the facts and rules. Hence, the rule-based system may involve giving inferences with some degree of error. The rule-based approach is the basis of a wide-range of knowledge-based systems applications. Furthermore, there are many examples of rule-based decision-support systems being successfully used by organizations [JHGJ88, And89, RS91].

7.2.1 Production rules

One of the early developments in artificial intelligence was the representation of knowledge in the form of production rules. These are often described as "If...Then" rules and are of the following form.

IF *condition*$_1$ and ... and *condition*$_n$ THEN *conclusion*

For example, a useful rule for *sid* is the following.

IF *sid hears the weather report and it predicts rain*
THEN *sid takes an umbrella when leaving home*

Rules can be straightforwardly used for a range of situations, for instance as follows, where X and Y might be composed from a number of variables and predicates.

IF X is the scenario
THEN Y is an appropriate action

IF X are the symptoms
THEN Y is the diagnosis

IF X is the situation
THEN Y is the prediction

IF X are the observations
THEN Y is the hypothesis

IF X are the preconditions
THEN Y is the action

Much knowledge used by humans in problem solving can be formulated in the form of rules. Disparate application areas such as medicine, finance, and design, are being found to be amenable to modelling using production rules.

To use production rules, some form of manipulation is necessary. This is undertaken by an inference engine, and is used to derive conclusions from rules. Once a conclusion has been derived, it can be added to the set of data, and then used in the derivation of further conclusions. This kind of inference mechanism is a data-driven approach. Given some production rules and some data, consequences of the data can be determined. This approach is also known as the forward-chaining approach.

A disadvantage of this approach is that a vast number of conclusions may be derived before a conclusion of interest is derived. A contrasting approach, that does not suffer from this problem is that of the goal-directed approach. Given some production rules and some data, a goal is satisfied, or derivable from the production rules and data, if the goal is a member of the set of data, or if there is a rule in the set of production rules that has a conclusion that matches with the goal, and has its condition satisfied as a sub-goal. This approach is also termed the backward-chaining approach. Given a goal, backward-chaining continues until all goals are eventually satisfied, or until it fails.

In rule-based systems, more than one rule can have the same consequent. Furthermore, more than one conclusion can be derived by the same condition. More sophisticated rule-based systems incorporate some form of conflict resolution strategy to decide which rule to select. A conflict resolution strategy can be based on criteria such as using the most recently added rule first; using the rules in some strict rotation; and using the most specific rule first. Unfortunately many of these techniques are *ad hoc*, and therefore applications using them require careful development by knowledge engineers.

Much of the research, and hence much of the literature, into expert systems has been on the rule-based systems approach. A key prototype was the MYCIN system [Sho76], from which many decision-support systems have been derived, in particular commercial systems. Unfortunately, MYCIN lacks a sound theoretical basis and as a result suffers from some problems in inferencing, in particular with regard to its handling of uncertainty based on certainty factors [HH88]. For a review and critique of a range of other experimental rule-based systems that handle uncertainty see [Spi86b].

Formal approaches such as discussed in this text can be harnessed as a basis for rule-based systems. In the next subsection we indicate some of the options, and then in subsequent chapters provide examples.

7.2.2 Technology for rule-based systems

Reasoning with production rules can be viewed as a form of logical reasoning. Hence, we can use approaches including fuzzy logic and default logic.

Default rules of the following form capture information that if α holds, and it is consistent to believe β, then β holds.

$$\frac{\alpha \; : \; \beta}{\beta}$$

In this way, we can use the formal and well-understood machinery of default logic to form the basis of a rule-based system. Furthermore, we can use the full power of default rules, in the following form, to allow for blocking of default rules.

$$\frac{\alpha \; : \; \beta}{\gamma}$$

If $\neg\beta$ holds, then we cannot use this default. Alternatively, we can use one of the prioritized forms of default logic to provide an efficient form of conflict resolution [Bre91, Bre94].

In Chapter 5, we discussed inference engines for default logic. This is still a research area, and only prototype systems are currently available. As an alternative route to using default logic, there are some useful techniques for translating knowledge-bases of default rules into Prolog, which can be automated [DNP94].

Prolog is now an increasingly viable programming language for information systems [PAP94, PAP95]. There are some well supported commercial environments allowing for integration with various relational database packages, and various widely-used programming languages. These environments run on a wide range of platforms, offer efficient computation with knowledge-bases, and provide various knowledge engineering tools.

In Section 8.2, we consider the application of default logic in a knowledge-base for addressing the problems of incomplete information in databases, and section 9.3, we consider the application of default logic in a knowledge-base for information retrieval.

In Chapter 4, we discussed fuzzy logic for reasoning with conditional statements. The definition of the fuzzy logic connectives and of generalized modus ponens provides the machinery for implementing rule-based systems based on fuzzy logic [Zad83]. Fuzzy techniques have been used to develop fuzzy expert system shells, for example [UHT94], fuzzy Prolog [MSD89], a fuzzy Prolog database system [LL90], and a fuzzy programming language called FRIL [Bal87].

Pioneering applications for rule-based fuzzy logic have been made in control systems [Mam76, HO82]. Rule-based fuzzy logic has also been applied to decision support. We consider an application of fuzzy production rules to information retrieval in Section 9.4. For further information on a variety of applications of fuzzy sets and systems, see [DPY95, Fuz93, Fuz94b].

7.3   Case-based systems

There are problems with developing and using the rule-based approach in supporting decision-making, since it can be difficult to understand an application domain sufficiently well to be able to develop good rules. An alternative is to focus on solving problems by retrieving information on related past cases of the problem. This alternative is called case-based reasoning.

Key areas of application for case-based reasoning include medical diagnosis, machine diagnosis, legal reasoning, and problems in design [Kol91].

Case-based reasoning addresses problem-solving and reasoning tasks in domains where experience is strong, but where the domain model is either weak or not acceptable to the end-user. A case-base contains specific solutions or specific precedents that can be used to solve problems or support relevant chains of reasoning.

When a new problem or scenario is encountered, instances from the case-base are retrieved and adapted to address the situation at hand. Tasks that are appropriate for case-based reasoning are typically characterized by multiple solutions where the ability to compare different possibilities is more important than the notion of correctness.

For example, in a diagnostic system for a make of car, a number of cases of various malfunctions can be stored in a format that includes symptoms, further tests and repairs. So when a problem arises in a particular car, the closest matching previous cases can be retrieved and used by the mechanic to decide on the action to be taken.

Case-based reasoning systems typically provide for the following.

- Representation of cases in a repository.

- Organization of cases in an abstraction hierarchy.

- Access to cases through indexing and information retrieval.

- Conflict resolution across multiple cases.

- Adaptation of retrieved cases to current problem.

- Incorporation of new cases.

The key uncertainty problem with the case-based approach is the actual selection of relevant cases. The user specifies the area of interest using keywords, and the system has to interpret the keywords, and identify cases that are likely to be of relevance. In this way there is a significant overlap with problems of information retrieval, as discussed in Chapter 9. There are problems of precision (ensuring that a significant proportion of cases retrieved are relevant), and recall (ensuring that a significant proportion of the relevant cases are actually retrieved). Furthermore, the coverage in Chapter 9 indicates how formal approaches to uncertainty can be incorporated into case-based reasoning systems. For further information on case-based reasoning see [Kol91, Kol94].

7.4   Bayesian network systems

Bayesian networks have been applied to decision-support tasks such as diagnosis, fault analysis, risk assessment, and analysis, and they have been applied by a range of organizations. For example, Pathfinder is a major system based on Bayesian networks and has been marketed as an expert system for medical diagnosis [Hec91a]. In addition to decision-support, Bayesian networks have been used in a variety of other applications including information retrieval and information filtering which we cover in Chapter 9. The fundamentals of Bayesian nets were introduced in Chapter 3. Here, we focus on the technology.

Most significant packages for construction of model-based expert systems are based on the techniques discussed in Chapter 2. They incorporate probability-based deduction that is applicable to complex nets with cause-effect relations. An example is the Hugin system [AOJJ89] that incorporates a graphical editor for interactive construction, maintenance, and testing of knowledge bases represented by Bayesian networks and a compiler that transforms the network into a computationally efficient structure for reasoning. Another example is the Belief system [ABM94]

The Bayesian networks approach is particularly appropriate for applications where there is a lot of data that can be used to train the network. In other words, in situations where there is a lot of data, this data can be used to derive the relevant conditional probabilities [Bun95].

For applications where there might not be enough data to form a sufficiently accurate probabilistic model, or for applications where some abstraction of a Bayesian network is desirable, an approach based on qualitative probabilistic networks has been proposed [Wel88]. This approach is based on using the following type of inequalities.

$$P(\alpha \mid \beta \wedge \gamma) \geq P(\alpha \mid \neg\beta \wedge \gamma)$$

If this inequality holds, a node in a network corresponding to α is positively influenced by a node corresponding to β. Such qualitative influences, rather than explicit probability values, can be propagated and aggregated in the network in a way that is consistent with the axioms of probability theory. Whilst the reasoning is weaker than that of normal probabilistic reasoning, it can be useful.

Another probabilistic network approach to decision making is based on influence diagrams [Hol89, HBH91]. These are extensions of Bayesian networks in that they contain decision theory variables as well as chance variables. Using these variables, they can support decision analysis using utility theory. They therefore can take into account the relative risks of "losses" or likelihood of "gains" to result from the various decision options under consideration. For an introduction to utility theory see [Nor68, MMH+76, Sch86]. An example of a software package based on influence diagrams is Ideal [SB91].

7.5 Knowledge engineering

Knowledge engineering is the process of capturing knowledge on a domain and using it to develop a knowledge-based system. Furthermore, knowledge engineering issues have at least some impact on all the applications discussed in this book. However, knowledge engineering is in general not a straightforward exercise. Obtaining the required information might be difficult since it might not be documented. It also often involves representing and reasoning with complex information. These difficulties have impeded the development of knowledge-based systems, and as a result, it has been described as the knowledge engineering bottleneck [FM84].

7.5.1 Knowledge acquisition

In many knowledge-based systems for decision-support there is the need to base the system at least partly on the knowledge provided by domain experts. The process of obtaining this knowledge is called knowledge acquisition.

Consider developing an expert system that models decision making by an expert in a particular domain. Here, the aim is to identify the rules, or heuristics, the expert uses, and incorporate them in the model. Unfortunately, the domain expert might not be fully aware of the rules that he or she uses in practice. The expert might not be able to formulate them, some might be temporarily forgotten, and others might only by used subconsciously.

Clearly knowledge acquisition is usually a difficult task. It is a problem addressed by an inter-disciplinary research community including psychologists, cognitive scientists, operational researchers, software engineers, and management scientists. This has led to a variety of solutions in both tool support (see for example [Nea88]) and methods (see for example [D'A88]).

There are many knowledge acquisition issues with regard to capturing uncertain information in knowledge bases [GB91, CA91]. As an example, the acquisition of subjective probabilities can be facilitated by also using objective probabilistic information [SFB90, SGG93]. Important issues for knowledge acquisition and knowledge engineering include structuring and refining Bayesian networks [Pea86, Hen89, SRA90, Hec91b, GC91], and obtaining heuristics for rule-based systems [BG88a, BG88b].

Machine learning is also used as a tool to facilitate knowledge acquisition [GB90]. This includes techniques based on induction for developing logic programs [Mug92, Fla94], Bayesian networks [Bun95], and fuzzy values [GK95].

Other topics related to knowledge acquisition that we cover in this book are data fusion (Chapter 8) and systems engineering (Chapter 10). Part of the problem of data fusion is merging expert opinions. This is also a problem in knowledge acquisition. A key problem in systems engineering is developing consistent requirements analyses and specifications. This is particularly problematical when there are a number of participants each with their own needs and experience.

7.5.2 Knowledge reuse

Another angle on the knowledge-engineering bottleneck, is the proposal to reuse knowledge-bases [NFF+91]. For many potential applications, there are existing knowledge-based systems that are for the same or similar domains. Instead of building new knowledge-bases for every application, the aim is to incorporate existing knowledge-bases. This potentially reduces duplication of effort.

The basis of this proposal has been the development of the knowledge interchange format (KIF) together with associated infrastructure and technology. This proposal has raised a number of research issues including:

- Translations between different knowledge representation formalisms.

- Communication protocols between different knowledge-bases, so that instead of merging a collection of knowledge-bases into one knowledge-base, the knowledge-bases can query each other.

- Protocols to minimize syntactic mismatches within a knowledge representation formalism, so that for example, the relations *isa*, *isa-kind-of*, *subsumes*, and *parents*, are equivalent.

Whilst the argument for KIF has appealing features, the viability of the approach has been seriously questioned [Gin91]. With respect to uncertain information, there are many difficulties, and it is unlikely to lead to generally applicable formal solutions in the short term. For example, suppose we have one knowledge-base using probabilisitic information, and one using fuzzy information, there are no general principles, yet, for merging the information into one knowledge-base.

Perhaps more difficult is allowing the one knowledge-base to query the other. If the fuzzy information knowledge-base receives some inference such as the following from the probabilistic knowledge-base,

$$P(rain \mid black\text{-}clouds) = 0.8$$

how will the fuzzy information handle this kind of probabilistic information in a formal and consistent fashion?

Nevertheless knowledge reuse will definitely become an increasingly important research area in the near future, and we return to it in Chapter 8 with respect to data fusion.

An alternative to coupling knowledge-bases, as in KIF, is to adopt a central reusable knowledge-base, and then build new applications by augmenting this knowledge-base with further specific knowledge for the application. This is the approach of CYC, a large common-sense knowledge-base developed to be useful in a wide range of applications [GL90, LG90]. This knowledge-base contains information on diverse topics such as bank accounts, animals, transport, and so on. It includes information such as "animals live for a single solid period of time", "nothing can be in two places at once", and "animals don't like pain". Such information is not usually documented since it is too common. Yet for knowledge-based systems that are viable in applications, it can be very useful. Also, note how much of this kind of common-sense information is default information.

7.5.3   Integration with software engineering

Whilst some knowledge-based systems are used as stand-alone systems, many are embedded in larger information systems, such as those discussed in the following chapters. Therefore for new computer technologies such as default reasoning, probabilistic reasoning, or fuzzy reasoning, to gain acceptance in a commercial environment, it is essential that software engineering techniques are provided. This includes developing (1) tools to facilitate the modelling of the domain and capture of uncertain information applicable to the domain, and (2) methodological support for how the tools should be used.

To gain acceptance, it is necessary that the new technology can be utilized using the same techniques used to manage other software in the organization. This requires that the modelling languages provided are as far as possible simple modifications of existing modelling languages, such as entity-relationship or object-oriented modelling. For example, the common KADS conceptual modelling language is a development of conceptual modelling techniques extended to knowledge models [SWA+94]. As another example, in [MH96], standard data modelling techniques have been extended to handle default rules in databases. Clearly there is a need for similar techniques for using probabilisitic information, fuzzy information and inconsistent information in information systems.

7.6   Prospects in knowledge-based systems

Knowledge-based systems are increasingly important as decision-support systems, and as components within larger information systems such as executive information systems, work-group systems, workflow systems, and information retrieval systems. The predominant approach is rule-based, though case-based reasoning is increasingly used in decision-support applications.

Currently, the majority of knowledge-based systems incorporate little or no uncertainty reasoning capability. Furthermore, for rule-based systems, the dominant uncertainty approach is certainty factors. Whilst for small applications, the inherent problems of certainty factors can be avoided by careful engineering, larger applications require more sophisticated solutions. Hence, logical, fuzzy set, and probabilistic formalisms will be increasingly incorporated.

In case-based reasoning, there is much scope for applying uncertainty formalisms for addressing the problem of selecting cases, in particular, in indexing cases. A significant part of this problem is in reasoning about keywords. Here statistical, semantic, and syntactic, information is available for constructing appropriate reasoning systems. Much of the discussion in Chapter 9, where we examine the application of default, probabilistic, and fuzzy information to information retrieval and filtering, is relevant for case-based reasoning.

More generally much of the discussion in the following chapters is relevant to uncertainty in knowledge-based systems. In the next chapter, data completion, fuzzy querying, and data fusion, can be regarded as applications for knowledge-based systems. Similarly, in Chapter 9, the systems discussed for information retrieval and information filtering are knowledge-based systems. Finally, in Chapter 10, much of the discussion on merging viewpoints and handling conflicts is relevant to knowledge engineering and to developing expert systems that can support multiple expert opinions.

Chapter 8

Uncertainty in Database Systems

8.1 Introduction

Uncertainty in information affects databases in various ways. Possibilities include: (1) Missing data; (2) There is some associated uncertainty with known data, such as a probability value; and (3) Queries are uncertain, such as with fuzzy queries.

For missing data, there might be a need to use some marker, called a null value, that indicates the data is missing. Alternatively, there might be a need to use default information to derive a likely value for missing data and substitute it for a null value. This is known as data completion.

In addition to these uncertainties, there could be the need to merge different sets of data to form a single database. This is known as data fusion. Also, there could be the need to derive useful abstraction of data or to learn from data. This is known as data mining.

In this chapter we consider missing data, probabilistic databases, fuzzy databases, data fusion, and data mining. For each of these issues, we will make references to uncertainty techniques discussed in Chapters 3 to 6.

8.2 Missing data

Relational databases are central to the majority of information systems used today. They are ideal for handling "tables" of information when that information is certain. They have a well-understood theoretical basis, and are intuitive to develop and use. However, when data is missing, the onus is usually on the developer or user to adopt some strategy for dealing with the situation. To address this problem of missing data, the use of null values has become increasingly important. Here we briefly review null values, and consider them as a form of default information. We can extend the idea of using default information by allowing a wider range of default values to be used to substitute for missing information, and hence provide data completion.

8.2.1 Null values

Null values are required when an attribute in a row of a relation is missing. Hence, they are used to handle a form of incomplete information. The idea was proposed by Codd [Cod86], and can be used to represent statements such as "the value exists but is unknown", or "the value does not exist". A wide variety of proposals for null values have been made (for reviews see [Ull88, MR92, Dem95, Zic95]), and there has been some commercial uptake of these ideas.

Null values can be marked so that each missing item of data has a unique symbol or value. The same value may then have several occurrences in a database, and each occurrence can then refer to the same piece of data, even though this data is unknown. For example, suppose the same teacher teaches *french* and *german*, but the name of the teacher is unknown. In addition suppose there is a teacher called *john*, but it is unknown what he teaches. This can be represented by the following, where α_1 and α_2 are marked null values.

$$teaches(\alpha_1, french)$$
$$teaches(\alpha_1, german)$$
$$teaches(john, \alpha_2)$$

The idea can be extended to allow constraints on marked null values [DdC88]. So for example, the following constraint could be added to the above example.

$$\alpha_2 \neq mathematics$$

This constraint adds to the database the fact that the subject *john* teaches is not *mathematics*. This may constitute useful information for users of the database.

Recourse to null values is clearly dependent on the nature of the rest of the data and on the intended use of the data. This raises some interesting

110

opportunities if we consider the use of null values in the context of non-monotonic reasoning. The use of null values is actually non-monotonic. For example, in a personnel database, a new employee may have been appointed, but not assigned a task. A null value in the field for *office* could represent "not yet assigned". Eventually, the new employee will be assigned a task, and hence this null value will be updated. In this way, new information causes the default null value to be retracted.

Formalizing the use of null values in non-monotonic proof theory offers a formal framework for comparing and contrasting approaches. In addition it provides a means for automating their use. Since default information is often presented in the form of If...Then rules, it means the contexts in which each null value can be used can be specified explicitly in the database management system. So for example,

> IF attribute n is missing in row m of relation r
> THEN attribute n is the null value v in row m of relation r^*

where r^* is the completed relation for r, and the null value v could be some form of null value such as 'existing but not known'. Further conditions can be added to the antecedent of such default rules to take into account other attribute values in the row, or other rows for that attribute. Conditions can also be added to limit the contexts in which rules could be applied. Clearly, we can use default logic to formalize this kind of information.

8.2.2 Data completion

The approach of null values can be extended to the notion of data completion by using a wider variety of default values. For example a telephone company is unlikely to have information on whether each customer has teenage children, but from other information, such as telephone use profiles, it might be possible to identify some fairly accurate default rules. These rules could then be used to generate a completed database with default values on whether each customer does have teenage children. Such a completed database might then be of interest for marketing telephone services oriented to teenagers. The examples of default rules discussed in Section 5.2.1 are an obvious way of implementing data completion.

As another example, consider a bank that wants to examine its database records to determine which customers to mail regarding a new investment plan. Below is a default rule for this, where *otherwise-committed(Name)* holds for reasons such as the customer is about to buy a house.

$$\frac{savings(Name, Account, Balance)}{\wedge \; Balance > 10,000} : otherwise\text{-}committed(Name)}{send\text{-}investment\text{-}plan\text{-}mailshot(Name)}$$

Each of the predicates are defined in terms of data that might be available in a bank database, and information in the consequent of the default rule could be inserted into the database.

Obviously such rules can only be applied in certain applications. For example, consider our telephone company example again. Here it would be advantageous if the marketing department could create a completed database for the purposes of a mailshot, since there is a low risk or cost in having some errors. Whereas if the accounts department introduces errors in a completed database, then the risks and costs might be significant.

Another kind of data completion comes from the basic assumptions about the completeness of a given database. For some databases, it is reasonable to assume that all relevant information about a relation is in the database. For other databases this is not a reasonable assumption. Consider an airline database. It is reasonable to expect that all destinations for the airline are in the database, and that if a destination is not in the database, it is not a destination for that airline. This is called the closed world assumption, and is another form of non-monotonic reasoning [Rei78]. The simple alternative to the closed world assumption is the open world assumption. Here it is not assumed that all the relevant facts are in the database.

8.3 Probabilistic databases

There are a number of ways that probabilistic data can be incorporated into databases. Here we consider two ways of introducing probabilities, called type 1 probabilistic relations and type 2 probabilisitic relations [ZP95]. Essentially, type 1 has a probability attached to each tuple, indicating the likelihood the tuple is in the relation, whereas type 2 has a probability attached to some non-key attributes of each tuple. For a review of probability theory in databases see [Par96].

8.3.1 Type 1 probabilistic relations

A type 1 probabilistic relation extends the classical relation with a supplementary attribute that indicates that the tuple belongs to the relation. The probability attached to a tuple is assumed to be independent from that of other tuples. For example consider the following relation, where the first argument is a student, the second is a course, and the third is a probability value.

$$takes(michael, biology, 0.9)$$
$$takes(john, physics, 0.5)$$

So *michael* takes *biology* with probability 0.9, and hence, he doesn't take *biology* with probability 0.1. Similarly, *john* takes *physics* with probability 0.5 and he doesn't take *physics* with probability 0.5. We can consider this database reflects four possibilities.

Possibility 1 : $takes(michael, biology), takes(john, physics)$

Possibility 2 : $takes(michael, biology), \neg takes(john, physics)$

Possibility 3 : $\neg takes(michael, biology), takes(john, physics)$

Possibility 4 : $\neg takes(michael, biology), \neg takes(john, physics)$

Since, we know the probability of the elements of each possibility, we can calculate the probability of each possibility. Possibility 1 is 0.9×0.5, which is 0.45. Possibility 2 is 0.45. Possibility 3 is 0.05, and Possibility 4 is 0.05. Note that they add up to 1.

Conditional independence assumptions, such as between tuples or attributes, can oversimplify a model of the world. So for example, in the above database, the calculation might be significantly in error if *john* and *michael* are close friends who choose the same options.

Type 1 probabilistic relations can be formalized in probabilistic logics such as those discussed in Chapter 3. For further details see [ZP95].

8.3.2   Type 2 probabilistic relations

Type 2 probabilistic relations extend the idea of type 1 relations by allowing for probability values to be attached to values of non-key attributes. The key attributes are deterministic. For example, consider the following version of the relation *takes*. Here, the first argument is a student, and the second argument is a set of courses with a probability attached to each course.

$$takes(ann, [maths/0.7, design/0.3])$$
$$takes(mary, [electronics/0.4, chemistry/0.4])$$

113

The second argument is a set of exclusive values. For *ann*, she will take *maths* with probability 0.7, or *design* with probability 0.3. Similarly, *mary* will take *electronics* with 0.4, *chemistry* with 0.4, and neither with probability 0.2.

As for type 1 relations, we could ascertain the probability for each of the possibilities of this database. There are six possibilities.

Possibility 1 :   *takes(ann, maths), takes(mary, electronics)*

Possibility 2 :   *takes(ann, maths), takes(mary, chemistry)*

Possibility 3 :   *takes(ann, maths), takes no course*

Possibility 4 :   *takes(ann, design), takes(mary, electronics)*

Possibility 5 :   *takes(ann, design), takes(mary, chemistry)*

Possibility 6 :   *takes(ann, design), takes no course*

The probabilities for these possibilities are calculated as for the type 1 relations. So they are 0.28, 0.28, 0.14, 0.12, 0.12, and 0.06, respectively.

The exclusivity of values means that for example *ann* could not take both *maths* and *design*. This differs from type 1 relations where we could have the following example. Here, since the tuples are independent, *ann* could take both *maths* and *design*.

$$takes(ann, maths, 0.7)$$

$$takes(ann, design, 0.3)$$

Type 1 and type 2 probabilistic relations are just two of a range of possibilities for probabilistic databases. The formalization of type 1 relations in probabilistic logic should be possible for type 2. In addition, probabilistic logic could be used to suggest further options for extending relational databases to handle probabilistic data. For further information on type 2 probabilistic relations, see [BGMP92]. There is also a similar approach that supports a more comprehensive handling of incompleteness of probabilistic information [Lee92]. It is based on the Dempster-Shafer theory of handling probabilistic beliefs [Sha76].

8.4 Fuzzy databases

Fuzzy set theory can be used in a number of ways to widen the applicability of database systems. As a result fuzzy databases is a term that has been interpreted in a variety of ways. The coverage of fuzzy databases includes incorporating incompletely known or vague information into databases, modelling fuzzy concepts, as well as supporting flexible fuzzy query handling techniques. In this section we consider fuzzy data and fuzzy queries. See also Section 9.4 on fuzzy information retrieval. For a comprehensive review of fuzzy databases see [BP95, BK95, Par96].

8.4.1 Fuzzy data

As with probabilisitic data, a fuzzy value can be attached to each tuple [BZ84]. This value represents the grade of membership that the tuple has for the relation. However, there is more than one meaning for this value: For example, the value could represent the degree to which the tuple is a good example of the relation, or it could represent the certainty of the tuple. Consider the following example.

$$likes(john, honey, 0.9)$$

The attached value could indicate that the tuple (*john, honey*) is a good example of the relation *likes*. Alternatively, it could mean we are highly confident, or nearly certain, that *john likes honey*.

Another way of incorporating fuzzy values is to attach them to attributes. For example, for a database on used cars, the price might not be precisely known. This uncertainty could be handled by attaching a possibility value to the attribute.

8.4.2 Fuzzy queries

When querying a database, it can be desirable to avoid precise conditions for specifying the query. For example consider the following query.

Give me the names of inexpensive hotels near the railway station

Here there are the fuzzy terms *inexpensive* and *near*. These kinds of terms can be modelled using fuzzy sets, in a context sensitive way. In addition, it is likely that there will be a need for linguistic modifiers, such

115

as *very*, *more or less*, and *not too*, to update fuzzy membership functions. Modifiers can be defined as a function of a membership function, so for some membership function μ, *very* modifies this to μ^2. In this way, for example, the membership function for *expensive*, denoted $\mu_{expensive}$, can be modified by *very* to give the modified membership function $(\mu_{expensive})^2$.

Fuzzy querying can be applied to classical relational databases. This approach has resulted in fuzzy-SQL. The usual form of querying SQL is the following.

Select *attributes* from *relations* where *condition* holds

Essentially, fuzzy-SQL allows fuzzy conditions in querying. Fuzzy conditions extend the usual form of SQL conditions. These take an n attribute relation and forms an n+1 attribute relation, where the extra attribute is in the range (0,1), and represents the fuzzy membership for the tuple in the relation with respect to the fuzzy condition.

For example, consider the fuzzy membership function "middle-age" in Figure 4.1, and the relation schema *staff*(*Name*, *Age*) in the following query.

Select	*Name*
From	*Staff*
Where	*middle-age*(*Age*)

In this query, each tuple in the staff relation is transformed to incorporate a value for fuzzy membership that reflects the degree to which the tuple satisfies the fuzzy condition — the degree to which the age is middle-age. Queries can incorporate more than one such fuzzy transformation. They can also include fuzzy modifiers, such as *very*, fuzzy comparisons, such as "about equal to", and fuzzy set operators.

Since select can result in a number of tuples being returned that only differ in the fuzzy membership attribute, select can be qualified to return only tuples above a certain threshold, or only return the highest n tuples.

The flexibility of fuzzy-SQL can allow for more natural queries to be constructed. It also can be more efficient to use. For a comprehensive introduction to fuzzy-SQL see [BGH88].

8.5   Advanced techniques for databases

Two key issues in using databases in organizations are the rapidly increasing size of databases and the need to use data from heterogeneous sources. In

·this section we discuss these issues, and indicate some of the applications of uncertainty formalisms to them.

8.5.1 Data mining

The rapidly increasing size of databases in organizations is partly a problem of information overload. In other words, there is so much information being used in organizations that it is difficult to use it efficiently. This raises the question of whether the information can be handled in a more efficient way. One possible solution is to use abstractions of the information such as useful patterns or trends in the information. However, it is not only a problem, for some organizations it can be an opportunity. Since some organizations already use their information efficiently, deriving useful abstractions from the data is a way obtaining extra value from databases. The process by which abstractions are derived is called data mining.

The aim of data mining is the non-trivial extraction of implicit potentially useful information from databases. This is usually by some form of induction on a sufficiently large set of data. It is a frontier topic in which machine learning techniques are applied to database systems. The topic is known by other names including knowledge discovery, knowledge extraction, data pattern processing, and information harvesting [FPSM91].

In a typical data mining system, a discovery method undertakes the following tasks.

- Selection of focus of interest guided by domain knowledge and user preferences.

- Search of potentially interesting data for patterns.

- Evaluation of how interesting a pattern is based on statistical significance and user-defined biases.

- Presentation of findings in a human-oriented form.

For example, in a credit card company database, data on spending will be available. Here relationships between the number and type of air tickets bought per year could be compared with other kinds of expenditure. For example, there might be a relationship between people who buy first class tickets and their likelihood of buying opera tickets. Such a relationship could be very interesting for a marketing organization. This relationship could be presented as follows.

> *If customer X buys Y first class tickets per year*
> *and $Y > 3$*
> *Then customer X buys Z opera tickets per year*
> *where $Z > 10$.*

There are a variety of approaches to defining discovery methods. Many approaches are derived from machine learning techniques. Statistical techniques are also important. Furthermore, the role of uncertainty formalisms, as discussed in this book, is increasing. Currently, the use of probabilistic information is important, and the use of fuzzy information is increasing. In addition, it is likely that the role of default information will increase, particularly given that there is a demand for information to be presented as heuristics.

A number of methodologies, algorithms and tools are now available for data mining [Uni96]. For more details on data mining see [FU95, FPSSU96].

8.5.2 Data fusion

The need to combine information from multiple sources arises in various applications including: (1) Fusion of information from sensors, where imperfect measurements are taken and need to be aggregated; (2) Fusion of information from multiple datasets; and (3) Fusion of multiple expert opinions. The process of combining information from multiple, heterogenous, sources is called data fusion. In Chapter 10, we discuss the more general problem of handling multiple, possibly inconsistent, expert opinions.

Within organizations the motivation for data fusion arises for many reasons ranging from rationalization or mergers, where different databases need to be amalgamated, to organizations seeking more or better information that comes from a wider variety of sources. Merging heterogeneous databases is arising with increasing frequency. The kind of merging required ranges from forming a single new database from a collection of databases, to being able to answer user queries from a collection of databases. Some of the problems of merging have been addressed in distributed database management (for a review see [Ull88]) and federated database systems (for a review see [SL90]). In all these situations, there could be conflicting, partially inconsistent information, obtained from heterogenous sources, having differing levels of reliability.

A significant open problem in data fusion is having systematic means for dealing with the conflicts that arise in the data. For example, consider a situation where two companies merge. To economize, they may wish to merge their customer databases. If they fortuitously have the same data model, then probably the major kind of data problem is when both databases have an entry for the same customer, but the values entered are not the same. One solution is to use defeasible rules to make a selection. The choice is not necessarily difficult. For example, a preference for the more recent data could be used. It could also involve identifying that different values are semantically equivalent, such as *Road* and *Rd.* However, if they don't have the same data model, then the problem is likely to require more complex default information to resolve.

As another example, consider the problem of merging information coming from a number of online information systems, and suppose the information system can only accept queries from the user, and then process them by asking one or more online sources. In other words the data fusion system has little control over the online systems. Now if there is a conflict between information sources, how does the information system cope? One option is to again use default rules to select.

However, it seems that there is not a unique form of data fusion that would be adequate for all situations. This is unsuprising given that the types of uncertainty are diverse. The techniques developed so far are predominantly for fusion of information that has a single (homogeneous) type of uncertainty, such as inconsistent information [Cho94], probabilistic information [SK94], and fuzzy information [DP94].

8.6 Prospects in databases

Uncertainty formalisms can help to extend, in a systematic fashion, the kinds of information used in a database, and to extend the kinds of querying. They can also be used to develop more advanced techniques such as data fusion and data mining.

Some of the ideas presented in this chapter, such as null values, are already being used by organizations, and it is likely that this usage will increase. It is also likely that this usage will extend into more advanced forms of data completion, perhaps based on a form of default logic.

Data mining is already making an impact with organizations keen to better information from their data warehouses. This is likely to increase markedly. Probabilistic databases, fuzzy databases and data fusion are also likely to be valuable technologies in the near future.

Another area of particular importance is the integration of knowledge-

119

base and database management systems [Ull88, Ker90]. The knowledge-base information retrieval systems discussed in the next Chapter are examples of such integration. Another increasingly important example is "data scrubbing". In this knowledge-base systems are used to check for imperfections in a database, such as identifying rows in a table that are redundant because they actually refer to the same entity (for example a pair of customer records where one has the name *Ann Smith* and the other has the name *Anna Smith* but they have the same age and address). More generally, integrating knowledge-base and database systems can extend a database with the implicit data available from the knowledge-base, and extend a knowledge-base with the large number of facts made available by the database. As an example, a default logic knowledge-base can be used to generate default intensional relations for a relational database [CEG94].

Chapter 9

Uncertainty in Online Information Systems

9.1 Introduction

There are a series of promising applications of uncertainty reasoning technology in online information systems. These include,

- Classifying incoming emails according to type or urgency.

- Filtering useful messages from newsgroups.

- Retrieving items from a database of newspaper articles and reports.

- Merging online information feeds.

- Routing messages in a work-group system.

In each of these kinds of application, there is uncertainty about the contents of the information, and about the best way of handling that information whether that handling involves filtering, retrieving, merging, or routing.

For each application, there is the opportunity to develop knowledge-bases on the application domain that can provide the information system with a "deeper" understanding of the information being handled. This can then be used to provide more sophisticated handling. For example, consider classifying short email messages. Here we can assume that each message has keywords extracted by well-known techniques (see for example [Sal89, FBY92]), and that these keywords can then be used by a knowledge-base to ascertain the type, urgency, etc. Knowledge-bases for these kinds of tasks can be generated from knowledge acquired from machine-readable dictionaries, lexicons, and thesauri, in addition to using usual rule-based systems development techniques.

In the following, we consider some of these options in more detail. As an example, we focus on the problems of information retrieval in Section 9.2. Then in Sections 9.3, 9.4 and 9.5, we discuss the application of default logic, Bayesian networks, and fuzzy logics respectively, to information retrieval, or filtering. In Section 9.6, we discuss how information filtering, indexing, and message routing, can be viewed as very similar problems to information retrieval.

9.2 Uncertainty in information retrieval

Information retrieval involves uncertainty. In an information system, the user is not certain about the contents of the information system, and the system is not certain about the user's needs. Information retrieval is about bridging this gap [TC95].

The aim of information retrieval is to provide a user with the "best possible" information from a database. The problem of information retrieval is determining what constitutes the best possible information for a given user. A common form of interaction for information retrieval is for the user to offer a set of keywords. These are then used by the information retrieval system to identify information that meets the user's needs. For example, in a bibliographic database, a user might be interested in finding papers on some topic. The keywords would be an attempt to delineate that topic. This then raises key issues of precision (ensuring that a significiant proportion of the items retrieved are relevant to the user) and recall (ensuring that a significant proportion of the relevant items are retrieved).

9.2.1 Statistical analysis versus semantic analysis

In order to determine how well matched an item in a database is for a query, most formal approaches to modelling the uncertainty in information retrieval use statistical information about keywords in the database. For example, a keyword in common between an item and a query, that occurs more in the item than in any other item, is a distinguishing feature of that item, and hence can increase the posterior probability that the item is of relevance to the user. A variety of such discriminating factors based on statistics have been proposed to quantify the similarity between items and queries (see for example [Sal89, vR79].

A great advantage of using statistical analysis is the volume of data that can be used to identify statistical relationships. For example, consider the amount of data in a bibliographic database for a university library or in a text database of past editions in a newspaper editorial office.

Using probability theory has proven to be of significant value, and a variety of interesting proposals have been made including the probability ranking principle [Rob77], and the binary independence model [vR79].

In statistical analysis, the relationship between keyphrases is established by frequency ratios, whereas in semantic analysis, the relationship is established by "meaning". Not using semantic information is wasting valuable information that could be critical in matching a user's needs to the information in the database.

For example, suppose a search is undertaken using the keyword *car*, it would miss all items that only have the keywords *automobile* and *motor-car*. Similarly, suppose a search is undertaken using the request *computer-network or academic-communications*, an excessive number of items might be retrieved, whereas what might have been actually of interest to the user was the more specialized subject *internet*.

Therefore, what is required is some formal representation of the semantic interrelationships between concepts, together with some ability to interpret users intended meanings when presenting requests.

9.2.2 The need for more than a thesaurus

Thesauri are widely-used tools in information retrieval for representing semantic information about keywords. Essentially, a thesaurus is a database, where for each keyword there is a listing of synonyms, more specialized keywords, more general keywords, and related keywords. Usually they are not automated tools. Rather they are used directly by the user for consultation, with the onus being on the user to interpret and utilize the information in the course of composing a request.

In order to capture semantic information more fully in information retrieval, we need to automate the information in the thesaurus. In addition, we need more sophisticated information. In particular, we need context sensitivity. For example, suppose we have the keyword *car*, then usually we would usually be interested in the synonym *automobile*. An exception would be if we also had the keyword *railway*. In which case we would usually be interested in the synonym *wagon*.

Thesauri lack an adequate representation of context dependency, and this is one way in which there is a shortfall for automation of thesauri. For automating the use of semantic information, we need to be able to specify when any particular specialization, generalization, synonym, or related term for a keyword can be used. Furthermore, we need to be able to extend this to resolving ambiguity such as arising from polysemes (words that have more than one meaning).

9.2.3 Formalisms for semantic information

There have been attempts to use knowledge-based systems to provide semantic analysis of keywords in information retrieval [Cro93, VV93]. For example, using the stems of words is widely acknowledged as improving performance, but it can introduce ambiguities. For example, consider the word *gravitation* which has the stem *gravity*. Here important semantic information is lost when the stem is used, since *gravitation* refers to the physics sense of *gravity*, whereas *gravity* could also have the sense of seriousness. Using a context-sensitive (semantic-sensitive) knowledge-base about word meanings can minimize these ambiguities being introduced [Kro93]. As another example, when sufficient contextual information is available in a request, disambiguation of keywords using a semantic network can be important in improving performance, and is likely to be even more important for diverse subject matter [Voo93].

Semantic techniques have also been used to enhance statistical techniques. For example thematic roles (from linguistic analysis) have been used to semantically categorize words in a query. This together with an extension of a probabilistic similarity function between queries and items [WD91] has provided a richer, finer-grained, statistical analysis.

None the less, there is a need for a more general framework for representing and reasoning with semantic information in information retrieval. Previous approaches to semantic analysis in information retrieval are either *ad hoc* representation schemes, insufficiently general in their approach, or lack some desirable properties. However, it is possible to use (non-monotonic) logics to handle semantic information about keywords, and so to identify logical relationships between items and queries. Even though many questions about using logics remain, we discuss the use of default logic in more detail in the next subsection.

There have been a number of other approaches to developing a logical framework for information retrieval including [vR86, CC92, Nie92, MSST93, BH94]. Some of these alternatives integrate logical and probabilistic features.

9.3 Default logic for information retrieval

In this section, we present a framework, based on default logic, for capturing semantic information about keywords [Hun95].

9.3.1 Keyphrases for items and requests

Let $\mathcal{K}$ be the usual set of formulae formed from a set of propositional letters and the connectives $\{\neg, \vee, \wedge\}$. A literal is any atomic proposition or its negation. We call $\mathcal{K}$ the set of keyphrases, and call any positive literal in $\mathcal{K}$ a keyword. The item keyphrase is a conjunction of literals. Intuitively this means the item contains information relating to each positive literal, and does not contain information relating to each negative literal. The request keyphrase is a specification by the user of what is of interest, and can be any formula in $\mathcal{K}$.

A factor in deciding whether an item is of interest to a user, is whether the item keyphrase classically implies some or all of the request keyphrase. For example, take the item keyphrase α, and the request keyphrase $\alpha \vee \beta$, then the item would be of interest by this factor.

The choice of keyphrase can affect the recall and precision of the retrieval. A keyphrase might be based on concepts too general, or too specialized, or may fail to incorporate important synonyms. For each keyphrase, it is important to consider whether a more general, or specialized keyphrase should be used, or whether it should be used with some synonym, or even replaced by some synonym. We call this reasoning activity "positioning".

9.3.2 Positioning for keyphrases

In order to formalize positioning for an item keyphrase, we assume semantic information is represented as a set of default rules. For this, let $\mathcal{L}$ be the set of predicates formed as follows: If α is a literal in $\mathcal{K}$, then $in(\alpha)$ is in $\mathcal{L}$ and $out(\alpha)$ is in $\mathcal{L}$. Intuitively, $in(\alpha)$ is an argument for α being in the positioned keyphrase, and $out(\alpha)$ is an argument for α not being in the positioned keyphrase. We form the usual set of formulae from $\mathcal{L}$ and the connectives $\{\neg, \wedge, \vee\}$. We then form the default rules from $\mathcal{L}$ as usual.

For a default database (D,W), D is some set of default rules and W is the smallest subset of $\mathcal{L}$ such that if α is a literal in the item keyphrase, then $in(\alpha)$ is in W.

For positioning, two important types of default rules are expansion and contraction. Expansion, of which the following is an example, intuitively states that if there is an argument for α being in the positioned keyphrase, and it is consistent to believe $in(\gamma)$, then there is an argument for γ being in the positioned keyphrase.

$$\frac{in(\alpha) : in(\gamma)}{in(\gamma)}$$

Contraction, of which the following is an example, intuitively states that if there is an argument for α being in the positioned keyphrase, and it is consistent to believe $out(\gamma)$, then there is an argument for γ not being in the positioned keyphrase.

$$\frac{in(\alpha) : out(\beta)}{out(\gamma)}$$

The positioned keyphrase is generated as follows, where E is an extension generated as usual from (D,W).

$$keywords(E) = \{\alpha \mid in(\alpha) \in E \wedge out(\alpha) \notin E\}$$

This says that if $in(\alpha)$ is in E, and $out(\alpha)$ is not in E, then α is in $keywords(E)$. If $keywords(E) = \{\alpha_1, .., \alpha_i\}$, then the positioned keyphrase is $\alpha_1 \wedge .. \wedge \alpha_i$. In this way the arguments "for" and "against" some α being in the positioned keyphrase are such that the arguments against α take precedence over arguments for α. In other words, if we have $in(\alpha)$, and $out(\alpha)$, then $out(\alpha)$ wins, and hence α is not in the positioned keyphrase.

For example, suppose in a database of newspaper articles, we had an article with the item keyphrase, $mexico \wedge usa \wedge trade$. A reasonable generalization could be captured by the following expansion default rule.

$$\frac{in(trade) \wedge (in(mexico) \vee in(usa) \vee in(canada)) : in(nafta)}{in(nafta)}$$

Assume the default theory (D,W) where D is the above default, and W is $\{in(mexico), in(usa), in(trade)\}$. Since $in(trade) \wedge (in(mexico) \vee in(usa) \vee in(canada))$ follows classically from W, and $in(nafta)$ is consistent with W, and the consequents of the defaults applied, then $in(nafta)$ holds. Hence the positioned keyphrase becomes $mexico \wedge usa \wedge trade \wedge nafta$. In this example, we have positioned by using only one default rule. In practice, we would require many default rules.

Once we have positioned a keyphrase, we can retrieve items from the database. Let $\mathcal{I}$ be some set of identification numbers for items, and $\mathcal{K}$ is the set of keyphrases. Let $\mathcal{R}$ be the set of pairs $(n, \beta_1 \wedge .. \wedge \beta_i)$ where $n \in \mathcal{I}$ and $\beta_1, .., \beta_i$ are keywords in $\mathcal{K}$. Each keyword denotes a class in which the item n is a member, and so n is in the intersection of $\beta_1, .., \beta_i$.

To retrieve items, we assume two forms of retrieval defined as follows, where $\Delta \subseteq \mathcal{R}$, and $(n, \beta) \in \mathcal{R}$. Let α be a request keyphrase, and let β^* be the positioned version of the item keyphrase β.

$$\{n \mid (n, \beta) \in \Delta \text{ and } \beta \vdash \alpha\}$$

$$\{n \mid (n, \beta) \in \Delta \text{ and } \beta^* \vdash \alpha\}$$

The first definition is classical, or Boolean, retrieval. The second is an amended form of Boolean retrieval that uses the positioned keyphrase. For both definitions, an item is retrieved only if its keyphrase completely covers the request keyphrase.

9.3.3   Types of positioning

For a keyphrase β, we consider three types of positioning. These are defined, using the classical consequence relation $\vdash$, as follows, where β^* is the positioned keyphrase.

$$\text{(Strengthening) } \beta^* \vdash \beta \text{ and } \beta \nvdash \beta^*$$

$$\text{(Weakening) } \beta^* \nvdash \beta \text{ and } \beta \vdash \beta^*$$

$$\text{(Shifting) } \beta^* \nvdash \beta \text{ and } \beta \nvdash \beta^*$$

The intuitive nature of strengthening and weakening is clear. In shifting it is usually the case that there is some γ such that $\beta \vdash \gamma$ and $\beta^* \vdash \gamma$, and γ is only slightly weaker than both β and β^*. We show this by examples.

Suppose in our article database, we have an article with the item keyphrase, $in(olive) \wedge in(oil) \wedge in(cooking)$. A reasonable specialization could be captured by the following default rule.

$$\frac{in(oil) \land in(cooking) : in(\neg petroleum)}{in(\neg petroleum)}$$

Since $in(oil) \land in(cooking)$ follows classically from the item keyphrase, and $in(\neg petroleum)$ is consistent with the original item keyphrase, and consequents of the defaults applied, then $in(\neg petroleum)$ holds. So the positioned keyphrase becomes $olive \land oil \land cooking \land \neg petroleum$. This strengthening limits the ambiguity of the keyword *oil*, since the positioned keyphrase wouldn't be concerned with articles about *petroleum*.

Now suppose in our article database, we have an article with the keyphrase, *rail* ∧ *car*. Since *car* might not be regarded as an optimal keyword, the following could be useful.

$$\frac{in(rail) \land in(car) : in(wagon)}{in(wagon)} \qquad \frac{in(rail) \land in(car) : out(car)}{out(car)}$$

From this, the positioned keyphrase becomes *rail* ∧ *wagon*. This is an example of shifting, and in this case it is intended to limit the ambiguity of using the keyword *car*.

Finally, we consider an example of weakening. Suppose in our article database, we have an article with the item keyphrase *computer-networks* ∧ *internet*. Since there are now many articles on computer networks, it is perhaps better to focus on this article being about the internet. This can be achieved by the following default.

$$\frac{in(computer\text{-}networks) \land in(internet) : out(computer\text{-}networks)}{out(computer\text{-}networks)}$$

So given $in(computer\text{-}networks)$ and $in(internet)$, we obtain the relation $out(computer\text{-}network)$. Then by the definition of *keywords*, the relation $out(computer\text{-}network)$ takes precedence, and hence the positioned keyphrase becomes *internet*.

9.3.4 Obtaining default rules

In order to use default rules, we need a strategy for training (or generating) them. We outline an apporach here. Let Γ be a training set for deriving default rules. We regard the set of items (identification numbers) as a space that is divided by the classes generated by the keywords. Then we ask a user, or appropriate substitute, to consider this space of items and use their own keywords to classify the items. The default rules are derived from the mapping between how the item keyphrases classify the items, and how the user classifies the items.

For example, let Γ contain $(23, ford \land car)$, $(25, volvo \land car)$, and $(26, fiat \land automobile)$, and suppose the user classifies 23, 25, and 26 as *motorcar*. For this a default rule could be as follows.

$$\frac{in(car) \lor in(automobile) : in(motorcar)}{in(motorcar)}$$

We would then repeat this process for a number of users. This would allows us to capture a number of the synonyms, polysemes, and related terms that the users would expect when identifying items such as those found in the training set.

This process assumes that the training set is a reasonable approximation of the whole possible space of items. If not the default rules derived might cover an inadequate subset of the items, and furthermore, errors could be introduced. If there are significant examples missing, then exceptions to default rules might not be identified. This means default rules could be generated that could be applied in incorrect circumstances. The only guard against these problems is taking a sufficiently large training set and a sufficiently large number of users. What constitutes "sufficiently large" can only be estimated by repeated training and testing cycles. In this sense, there is a commonality with knowledge engineering and inductive learning issues.

9.3.5 Viability of default reasoning in information retrieval

The use of logic, and particularly default logic, offers a useful and lucid formalization of uncertainty between items and requests. In addition, statistical and syntactic information can also be presented as default rules.

Clearly, qualitative abstractions of statistical information about relationships between keywords can be used. For example, if there is a good correlation between a pair of keywords co-occuring in a set of documents, then we could represent this by a default equivalence between these two keywords. In other words, we could represent statistical relationships as heuristics. Indeed there is a growing interest in both the non-monotonic logic community and the machine learning community for using merging statisical techniques with the logical process of induction for the generation of non-monotonic hypotheses (for example see [CHS93]).

In addition, syntactical information is often of the form of heuristic rules, and hence can also be harnessed. To illustrate, consider that in English there are about 250 suffixes, and that heuristic rules can be identified for adding or removing these suffixes from words. Since a request keyword and item keyword might have the same stem, but different suffixes, they would not match without the heuristics to translate them into the same form. As with the semantic and statistical information, syntactical information is often context dependent. For example, (taken from [Kro93]), *suited* is reduced to *suit*, but *suites* is reduced to *suite*. In this way default logic can provide a formal framework for representing these kinds of rules and their exceptions.

9.4 Fuzzy logic for information retrieval

Another alternative for addressing problems in information retrieval and information filtering is fuzzy logic.

9.4.1 Applying fuzzy logic to information retrieval

Here we consider the RUBRIC (RUle Based Retrieval of Information by Computer) system [TSMD93]. This is a fuzzy production rule system. The rules model a hierarchy of retrieval topics (or concepts) and subtopics. By naming a single topic, the user automatically invokes a goal-oriented search of the tree defined by all of the subtopics that are used to define that topic. Much of the technology is based on fuzzy logic reasoning discussed in Chapter 4, and on the rule-based systems discussed in Chapter 7.

The lowest level of information used includes keywords, data about relative positions of keywords, and simple syntactic and semantic information. Sub-topics are defined in terms of this information using If...Then rules. Further sub-topics, and eventually topics, are then defined in terms of sub-topics, again using If...Then rules. Rules are either of the following form,

> IF the text contains evidence α
> THEN there is evidence to degree X that it is also about β

or of the following form.

> IF the text contains evidence α
> THEN there is evidence to degree X that it is also about β
> BUT IF ALSO the text contains evidence γ
> THEN there is evidence to degree Y, and not X, that is about topic β

The "BUT IF ALSO" is a modifier. So if the text contains evidence α and γ, then use the degree Y instead of the degree X. The idea behind this is that some evidence can modify the belief in a (sub-)topic, but on its own is insufficient to support or deny belief in a (sub-)topic.

The data other than keywords can affect the choice of sub-topics. For example, for the sub-topic *us-president*, the keywords *president* and *clinton* would have to occur in the same sentence. An informal example of a rule is the following.

IF the text contains the word *bomb*
THEN the text is about an *explosive-device* with degree 0.6
BUT IF ALSO the text contains the words *boxing-match*
THEN the topic is about an *explosive-device* with degree 0.3

RUBRICS role is to assign a weight to each item in the repository, where the weight reflects the belief that the item is relevant to the query. The weight is determined by propagating the uncertainty value through the tree defined by the rule-base. Consider the following example.

IF the text contains the word *kidnapping*
THEN the text is about *violent-act* with degree 1.0

IF the text contains the word *bombing*
THEN the text is about *violent-act* with degree 1.0

IF the text contains the word *killing*
THEN the text is about *violent-act* with degree 1.0

IF the text contains the word *dead*
THEN the text is about *violent-effect* with degree 0.5

IF the text contains the word *debris*
THEN the text is about *violent-effect* with degree 0.5

IF the text is about *violent-act*
THEN the text is about *violent-event* with degree 0.8
BUT IF ALSO the text is about *violent-effect*
THEN the topic is about *violent-event* with degree 1.0

IF the text is about violent-event
THEN the text is about *terrorism* with degree 0.7
BUT IF ALSO the text is about *assassination*
THEN the topic is about *terrorism* with degree 0.9

A range of many-valued calculi have been tried for propagating the beliefs in these networks. An interesting observation from the experiments in information retrieval with RUBRIC was that there appeared to be no objective factors for preferring one many-valued calculus over any other.

9.4.2 Viability of fuzzy logic for information retrieval

For information retrieval, the RUBRIC approach, and hence more generally fuzzy logics, have been shown to be highly viable through experimentation. Furthermore, several paradigmatic ways of using evidence in information retrieval have been suggested [TSMD93].

In RUBRIC, evidence as a modifier has been exploited. Another possibility is evidence aggregation, where no single piece of evidence allows us to deduce the occurrence of a topic to any significant degree, but if there are several such pieces, then their effects are cumulative.

For another approach to the application of fuzzy reasoning in information retrieval see [GL93]. Also see Section 8.4 on fuzzy databases.

9.5 Bayesian networks for information retrieval

Given the vast amount of data that is usually available in an information retrieval system, the use of statistical or probabilistic information to enhance retrieval is appealing. Here we consider the application of Bayesian networks to information retrieval [TC91, FdF95].

9.5.1 Applying Bayesian networks in information retrieval

A viable approach to using Bayesian networks for information retrieval is based on the linking of two networks (see Figure 9.1). The first network, called the document network, is a representation of the documents, and is not changed for individual queries. The second network, called the query network, is a representation of the query and is specified for each query.

The document network is composed of document nodes and concept representation nodes. The query network has a root that captures the overall information requirement of the user. The query is defined in terms of query concepts, with intermediate query nodes, for multiple queries.

Links between the representation concepts and query concepts define the mapping between concepts used to represent the document collection and the concepts that make up the queries. In the simplest case, the query concepts are constrained to be the same as the representation concepts and each query concept has exactly one parent representation node. In general, this mapping also captures thesaurus information and domain knowledge about recognizing query concepts in documents.

Document nodes

Representation nodes

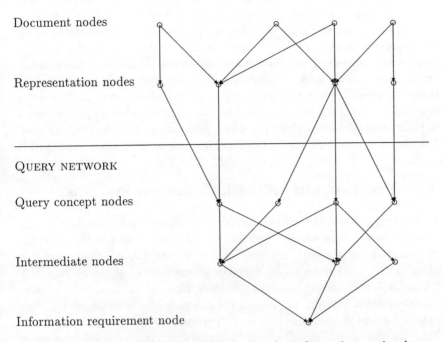

QUERY NETWORK

Query concept nodes

Intermediate nodes

Information requirement node

Figure 9.1: A Bayesian net architecture for information retrieval

Linking the query network with the document network does not affect the basic structure of the document network. None of the links nor conditional probabilities are modified. In this way, retrieval is an evidential reasoning process in which multiple sources of evidence about document and query content are combined to estimate the probability that a given document matches a query.

The approach can be used to simulate earlier probabilistic, Boolean, vector space, and cluster-based models [TC92]. Furthermore, these disparate models can be used concurrently, and their results aggregated to form an overall assessment of relevance within this framework.

9.5.2 Viability of Bayesian networks in information retrieval

The Bayesian network approach has been shown to allow significant improvements in retrieval performance at computational costs that are comparable to those for the commercial (Boolean) retrieval systems. The Bayesian network technology discussed in Chapter 7 can be used for this application.

From an engineering perspective, using probabilities is desirable given the amount of data available. Using Bayesian networks is particularly appealing as it offers a more efficient representation. In addition, background information can be used by providing an appropriate architecture for the Bayesian network. So for example, adopting the architecture in Figure 9.1 before considering the probabilistic information would allow a useful network to be developed more quickly than if only probabilistic information was used. For more discussion on developing Bayesian networks see Chapters 3 and 7.

9.6 Prospects in online information systems

We have emphasized the role of uncertainty handling in information retrieval. The problem of information filtering is actually very similar to that of information retrieval. Hence, the issues raised in Section 9.2, and the approaches of default logic, fuzzy logic and Bayesian networks discussed in Sections 9.3, 9.4 and 9.5, respectively, are highly relevant here.

Information filtering in online information systems is necessary when more information is coming to a user than the user needs or can cope with. Take for example, a newsfeed. Here many short messages are sent every minute. Obviously a reader cannot read them all, and hence some selection criterion, preferably automated, is required.

As another example, consider an email system for a busy administrator. Here, some emails could be filtered as requiring urgent attention, some could be redirected to subordinates, and some could be collected for when the administrator is less busy. As more information in the form of messages, articles, reports, and other kinds of documentation is communicated via online information systems, it is clear that there is an increasing need for sophisticated filtering technology.

Information filtering and information retrieval have been described as "two sides of the same coin" [BC92]. In both problems, there is an excessive amount of information to handle and there is an uncertainty gap between the user and the systems handling the information. Also, both rely on keywords offered by the user to select a subset of the information that could be useful to the user. Both need to identify keywords in the information and to reason with these keywords in order to ascertain the degree of match between each item of information and the request.

Clearly, semantic information as discussed in Sections 9.2 and 9.3, statistical information as discussed in Sections 9.2 and 9.5, and fuzzy information as discussed in Section 9.4, can be utilized. The probabilistic and fuzzy approaches might prove to be more valuable for information filtering where users' needs remain static than in information retrieval where usually new queries are constantly being generated. For example, consider an industry sector analyst monitoring newsfeeds. Here there would be a constant requirement to monitor certain companies, products, etc. Hence a query would be developed and improved over time.

As we indicated in the introduction, we believe that there is a wide range of applications that involve reasoning with textual information. Whilst in the long term, we can hope for versatile and robust natural language capability in software, in the short and medium term, we need to consider less sophisticated solutions that will be based on uncertainty handling techniques. Common to these applications will be the need to reason about semantic, syntactic, and statistical information about words and phrases in textual information. Users can present keywords to identify items such as items that are of interest or items that should be redirected. The reasoning will be necessary to gain some understanding of the textual information, and so to improve processes such as retrieving, filtering, classifying, routing, and merging information. The viability of applying uncertainty techniques to such processes is promising.

Chapter 10

Uncertainty in Systems Engineering

10.1 Introduction

The development of most large and complex systems necessarily involves many people, each with their own perspectives on the system defined by their knowledge, responsibilities, and commitments. Inevitably, the different perspectives of those involved give rise to the possibility of inconsistency between perspectives and to a need for co-ordination.

This leads to a need to tolerate inconsistencies in systems development, and more importantly to be able to act in a context-dependent way in response to inconsistency [FGH+94]. Here we consider a framework in which inconsistencies can be detected logically (using classical logic), and in which the information surrounding each inconsistency can be used to focus continued development [HN96].

Reasoning First, we address the notion of "tolerating inconsistency" by QC logic, that allows useful reasoning in the presence of inconsistency, as discussed in Chapter 6. The adaptation is a weakening of classical logic that prohibits all trivial derivations but still allows all resolvents of assumptions to be derived. We illustrate the use of the logic by some examples of multi-perspective development in which inconsistencies arise between different developers who hold different (inconsistent) views of a joint problem they are addressing.

Analysis We then address the need to analyse inconsistent specifications in the above setting. In particular, we propose the use of *labelled* QC logic which records and tracks information used in reasoning. We illustrate how the amended (labelled) proof rules of QC logic can be used to track inconsistent information by propagating these labels (and their associated information) during reasoning. We further demonstrate how specifications in labelled QC logic can be analysed in a variety of ways in order to gain a better understanding of the likely sources of inconsistencies that arise. Using this approach we can provide a "logical analysis" of inconsistent information. We can identify the likely sources of the problem, and use this to suggest appropriate actions. This "auditing" is essential if we are to facilitate further development in the presence of inconsistency.

Action Finally, we discuss the need, and present an approach, for acting in the presence of inconsistency. We suggest the use of meta-level rules of the form "inconsistency implies action", but emphasize that such inconsistency handling actions need not necessarily remove the inconsistency. Rather, action in this setting may include isolating, but not necessarily resolving, the inconsistency.

In this approach we can deal with inconsistent specifications in a way that allows us to analyse the likely sources of the inconsistencies, allows us to continue reasoning in a rational fashion in the presence of inconsistency, and provides a basis for acting on inconsistencies.

10.2 Information for developing specifications

Information that is manipulated in an evolving specification can be partitioned, and is often represented, in different ways. Since we assume that multiple development participants might be involved in a development process, this information is typically also distributed among these different participants. Development information includes:

Specification information about the actual system ("product") being developed. Such information can be captured as a collection of partial specifications denoted by loosely coupled, locally managed, distributable objects called "ViewPoints" [FKN+92].

Method information about the process of development and the representation schemes used to express partial specifications. This information also includes integrity constraints between representation schemes. This information can be captured as "inter-ViewPoint rules" [NKF94]. These rules describe relationships between representation schemes, and thus the relationships between partial specifications expressed using those representation schemes.

Domain information which is incrementally captured in an evolving specification process [EN95]. This information might pertain to the problem domain in which the system will be installed (and which is usually captured and represented separately). Alternatively, it might pertain to the solution domain (i.e., the product being specified), in which case it will be part of the specification information.

All three kinds of information described above (and represented as facts, rules, assumptions, graphs, etc.) can be translated into logical formulae, and inconsistencies can be detected logically. Additional assumptions can also be used to facilitate this inconsistency detection process. For example, the Closed World Assumption (CWA) can be used to make explicit negative information by adding the negation of certain facts, if those facts are not present in the specification.

10.3 Capturing development information in logic

Different kinds of development information can be translated into logical formulae which can then be handled in a uniform manner [FGH+94]. Translating software engineering specifications into logic facilitates the detection of inconsistencies and allows us to concentrate on reasoning about these inconsistencies. Furthermore, we believe that problems of translation are outweighed by the improvement in inconsistency management.

For many software engineering formalisms, classical logic can be used to capture specifications. However, we do not assume that there is a unique form for representing any given specification. Rather, there are usually obvious ways of presenting any specification as a set of logical formulae.

Consider, for example, an entity-relationship description of a bank (which is based on a set of nodes (denoting entities), and binary arcs (denoting relations between entities). We can easily capture such a representation scheme as illustrated by the following formulae.

139

$holds(bank, account)$

$has(customer, account)$

$\vdots$

$inheritance(cashier\text{-}transaction, transaction)$

The symbols *account*, *customer*, *transaction*, *cashier-transaction*, and *bank* are objects in the logic, the *holds*, *has*, and *inheritance* symbols are relations in the logic. In addition, we assume formulae that capture the special nature of certain relations such as the following.

$$\forall X, Y, Z\; inheritance(X, Y) \wedge inheritance(Y, Z) \rightarrow inheritance(X, Z)$$

Similarly, we can describe various constraints on our formalisms, such as the relationships between representation schemes or partial specifications. For example, consider the following simple rule for ensuring consistency of use of the syntax for multiplicity of association between two classes in an object model [RBP+91]. Assume the relations *has-exactly-one* and *has-exactly-two* between pairs of classes (for example, *has-exactly-one(son,mother)*). For these, we have the following rule.

$$\forall X, Y,\; has\text{-}exactly\text{-}one(X,\ Y) \leftrightarrow \neg has\text{-}exactly\text{-}two(X,\ Y)$$

Constraints can be useful as either specification information or domain information.

10.4 Reasoning in the presence of inconsistency

Here we focus on the problem of reasoning with information that might be inconsistent. By this, we mean the ability to continue development of a specification irrespective of any inconsistency in that specification, and irrespective of any inconsistency between that specification and some other related specification. We begin by briefly motivating the use of logic for performing such reasoning.

10.4.1 Classical logic for specifications

Classical logic is very appealing for reasoning with specifications. A variety of notations for representing specifications can be translated into classical logic, including Z specifications, ER diagrams, dataflow diagrams, and inheritance hierarchies. Furthermore, classical reasoning is intuitive and natural.

The appeal of classical logic, however, extends beyond the naturalness of representation and reasoning. It has some very important and useful properties which mean that it is well-understood and well-behaved, and that it is amenable to automated reasoning. First, there are a variety of proof theories and semantics, each with their own advantage. Second, the logic is decidable for the propositional case. This means that if we wish to know whether a particular formula holds in a specification, we can find this out in a finite number of steps. Third, the logic is semi-decidable for the first-order case. Whilst this is not as good as being decidable, it means that if a formula does follow from a specification, then we can find a proof in a finite number of steps. Furthermore, for both the propositional and first-order cases, it also means that we can construct a model of a consistent set of formulae, where a model is an assignment of truth-values to the atomic propositions in the formulae such that all the formulae are true according to the semantics of the logic.

In addition, there has been much progress in developing technology for classical reasoning. This includes automated reasoning systems for deriving inferences from sets of formulae [Fit90], and model building systems for giving models of consistent sets of formulae [CCB90, AC91].

10.4.2 Labelled QC logic

Labelled QC logic is a development of QC logic (discussed in Section 6.4) that is based on a labelled language. We use a labelled language to allow us to uniquely identify each item of development information. We propagate the labels by labelling consequences with the union of the labels of the premises. This means we can identify the ramifications of each item in the reasoning, since each inference will be labelled. Labels can be used to differentiate different types of development information and in particular they can indicate the sources of information. We demonstrate the utility of the labels later. Note that the idea of using a labelled language can be extended to other paraconsistent logics such as the weakly negative logics discussed in Section 6.2.

Let S be some set of atomic symbols such as an alphabet. If $i \subseteq S$, and $\alpha \in \mathcal{L}$, then $i : \alpha$ is a labelled formula. Let $\mathcal{M}$ be the set of labelled formulae. All development knowledge that we are analysing is translated into labelled formulae, where each formula has a unique label.

For example, let $S = \{a, b, c, ...\}$. Then examples of labelled formulae include the following.

$$\{a\} : holds(bank, account)$$

$$\{b\}: performs(cashier, transaction) \ \lor \ performs(atm, transaction)$$

There are many strategies that we could adopt for labelling development information. Options include combinations of the source of the item, and time the item was inserted. For this, some mapping from labels to their associated meaning needs to be recorded. For instance, different developers could use different disjoint subsets of the labels.

We obtain labelled QC logic by using only labelled formulae as assumptions, and by amending the proof rules to propagate the labels: The label of the consequent of a rule is the union of the labels of the premises of the rule.

Suppose we have the following development information, where a is a constraint, b is some domain knowledge, and c and d denote fragments of partial specification information.

$$\{a\} : \alpha \lor \neg\beta$$

$$\{b\} : \gamma \rightarrow \beta$$

$$\{c\} : \neg\alpha$$

$$\{d\} : \gamma$$

Clearly this development information is inconsistent. However, using the QC proof rules, we can obtain a number of non-trivial inferences. Consider the following proof.

Step 1 is $\{b\} : \neg\gamma \lor \beta$ from $\{b\} : \gamma \rightarrow \beta$
using arrow elimination

Step 2 is $\{b, d\} : \beta$ from $\{d\} : \gamma$ and Step 1
using resolution

Step 3 is $\{a, b, d\} : \alpha$ from $\{a\} : \alpha \lor \neg\beta$ and Step 2
using resolution

Step 4 is $\{a, b, c, d\} : \bot$ from $\{c\} : \neg\alpha$ and Step 3

In Step 2, we obtain the formula β that is labelled with $\{b, d\}$. This formula is non-trivial, and maybe useful for furthering the evolution of the specification. We show later how we use the label to qualify this inference. In qualifying an inference, we indicate the relationship between the data used for the inference and the inconsistent data in the development information: the closer the relationship, the more we qualify the inference.

In Step 4, we obtain the formula $\perp$ labelled $\{a, b, c, d\}$. The formula $\perp$ is an abbreviation for any inconsistent formula. The label tells us which parts of the development information have given the inconsistency. This label can be used for identifying the likely sources of an inconsistency, as discussed later.

10.5 Logical analysis of inconsistent specifications

So far we have seen how development information can be represented as logical formulae, and shown how we can undertake non-trivial reasoning with such formulae, even if they are mutually inconsistent. In this section we turn to logical analysis of inconsistent specifications. In particular, we consider qualifying inferences from inconsistent specifications, and identifying likely sources for an inconsistency. These are just two ways of providing a logical analysis of inconsistent specifications.

10.5.1 Qualifying inferences from inconsistent information

When considering inconsistent information, we have more confidence in some inferences over others. For example, we may have more confidence in an inference α from a consistent subset of the database if we cannot also derive $\neg \alpha$ from another consistent subset of the database.

Let Δ be a set of labelled formulae capturing development information. We form the following sets of sets of formulae, and let $CON(\Delta)$ be the set of consistent subsets of Δ, and $INC(\Delta)$ be the set of inconsistent subsets of Δ. If Δ is a set of labelled formulae capturing development information, then the function *Labels* is defined as follows.

$$Labels(\Delta) = \{i \mid i : \alpha \in \Delta\}$$

In the following definition, $MI(\Delta)$ is a set of sets of labels, where each set of labels corresponds to a set of minimally inconsistent formulae. A set of formulae is minimally inconsistent if every proper subset is consistent. Similarly, $MC(\Delta)$ is a set of sets of labels, where each set of labels corresponds

143

to a set of maximally consistent formulae. A set of formulae is maximally consistent, if the set is consistent and adding any further formulae to the set from Δ causes the set to be inconsistent.

Let Δ be a set of labelled formulae capturing development information, and let $\subset$ denote the strict subset relation, defined as follows: For X, Y, $X \subset Y$ if and only if $X \subseteq Y$ and $X \neq Y$. Also let $\not\subset$ denote the negation of the strict subset relation. We form the following sets of sets of labels.

$$MI(\Delta) = \{Labels(\Gamma) \mid \Gamma \in INC(\Delta) \text{ and } \forall \Phi \in INC(\Delta) \ \Phi \not\subset \Gamma\}$$

$$MC(\Delta) = \{Labels(\Gamma) \mid \Gamma \in CON(\Delta) \text{ and } \forall \Phi \in CON(\Delta) \ \Gamma \not\subset \Phi\}$$

$$FREE(\Delta) = \bigcap MC(\Delta)$$

We can consider a maximally consistent subset of a database as capturing a "plausible" or "coherent" view of the database. For this reason, the set $MC(\Delta)$ is important in many of the definitions presented in the next section. Furthermore, we consider $FREE(\Delta)$, which is equal to $\bigcap MC(\Delta)$, as capturing all the "uncontroversial" information in Δ. In contrast, we consider the set $\bigcup MI(\Delta)$ as capturing all the "problematic" data Δ. Note, $\bigcap MC(\Delta)$ is equal to $Labels(\Delta) - \bigcup MI(\Delta)$. So reasoning with $FREE(\Delta)$ is equivalent to revising the database by removing all the "problematic" data. This means we have a choice. We can either reason with the data directly using $FREE(\Delta)$ or we can revise the data by removing the formulae corresponding to $\bigcup MI(\Delta)$.

We now use these concepts to define three qualifications for an inference from inconsistent information. The approach is based on argumentative logics [EGH95]. Let Δ be a set of labelled formulae capturing development information, and let $i : \alpha$ be a labelled QC from Δ. We form the following qualifications for inferences.

α is an existential inference if $\exists k \in MC(\Delta)$ such that $i \subseteq k$

α is a universal inference if
$\forall k \in MC(\Delta)$ such that $j \subseteq k$ and $j : \alpha$ is a labelled QC inference from Δ

α is a free inference if $i \subseteq FREE(\Delta)$

So a formula is an existential inference if it is an inference from a consistent subset of the database. A formula is a universal inference if it is an inference from each maximally consistent subset of the database, whereas a formula is a free inference if it is an inference from the intersection of the maximally consistent subsets of the database.

If α is a free inference, it is also a universal inference. Similarly, if α is a universal inference, it is also an existential inference. Clearly, if α is only an existential inference, then we are far less confident in it than if it was a universal inference. If it is a free inference, then it is not associated with any inconsistent information. Consider the following assumptions.

$$\{a\} : \alpha \wedge \beta$$

$$\{b\} : \neg\alpha \wedge \beta$$

$$\{c\} : \gamma$$

This gives two maximally consistent subsets.

Set 1	Set 2
$\{a\} : \alpha \wedge \beta$	$\{b\} : \neg\alpha \wedge \beta$
$\{c\} : \gamma$	$\{c\} : \gamma$

From this, α and $\neg\alpha$ are only existential inferences, whereas γ is a free inference, and β is universal inference.

These kinds of qualification are useful when reasoning with inconsistent information because they provide a relationship between the inferences and the problematic data. We might feel happier about relying on the less qualified inferences. Furthermore, they provide a useful vocabulary for participants in the development process to discuss the inconsistent information.

10.5.2   Identifying likely sources of an inconsistency

When we identify an inconsistency in our development information, we want to analyse that inconsistency before we decide on a course of action (for example, further reasoning, removing inconsistency, etc.). Using labelled QC reasoning, we can obtain the labels of the assumptions used to derive an inconsistency. We use the term "source" to denote the subset of the assumptions that we believe to be incorrect. Suppose we have the specification.

145

$$\{a\} : \alpha$$

$$\{b\} : \neg\alpha \vee \neg\beta$$

$$\{c\} : \beta$$

and suppose $\{a\} : \alpha$ and $\{b\} : \neg\alpha \vee \neg\beta$ have been a stable and well-accepted part of the specification for some time, and by contrast $\{c\} : \beta$ is just a new and tentative piece of specification. Then for the inconsistency $\{a, b, c\} : \bot$, we could regard $\{c\} : \beta$ as the source of the inconsistency.

Identifying the source facilitates appropriate actions to be invoked. We discuss this further below and discuss "acting on inconsistency" in the next section. Let Δ be a set of labelled formulae capturing development information, and let i be some label of some inference from Δ. The set of assumptions from Δ corresponding to the label is defined as follows.

$$Formulae(\Delta, i) = \{j : \alpha \in \Delta \mid j \subseteq i\}$$

For an inconsistency $i : \bot$, $Formulae(\Delta, j)$ is a possible source of the inconsistency if $j \subseteq i$ and $Formulae(\Delta, i - j) \in CON(\Delta)$. Essentially, $Formulae(\Delta, j)$ is a possible source of the inconsistency if it corresponds to a subset of the assumptions used to obtain the inconsistency, and the remainder of the assumptions are consistent.

There may be a large number of possible sources of an inconsistency, and a number of options for addressing this, such as working only with the smallest sources, or working with only the sources that have the least effect on the number of inferences from the specification. However, if we are to act on inconsistency, then we really need to identify the "likely" sources of inconsistency. To address this, we assume that for any development information, there is some ordering over that information, where the ordering captures the likelihood of the information being erroneous. So, if i is higher in the ordering than j, then $i : \alpha$ is less likely to be erroneous than $j : \beta$.

An ordering is transitive if and only if when i is more preferred than j, and j is more preferred than k, then i is more preferred than k. An ordering is linear if and only if for any pair i and j, one of the following hold: (1) i is more preferred than j; (2) j is more preferred than i; or (3) i and j are equally preferred. We assume that the ordering over development information is transitive. It may also be linear.

If we assume there is an ordering over assumptions, then a more likely source is the smallest possible source that contains less preferred assumptions. Returning to the previous example, we can use explicit ordering to formalize this reasoning. For the specification above, $\{a\} : \alpha$ and $\{b\} : \neg\alpha \vee \neg\beta$ are both ordered higher than $\{c\} : \beta$. Hence β is a likely source.

Obviously, this approach does not guarantee that a likely source can be uniquely determined from a set of possible sources. Consider the following data,

$$\{a\} : \gamma$$

$$\{b\} : \beta$$

$$\{c\} : \neg\alpha$$

$$\{d\} : \beta \rightarrow \neg\alpha$$

where a, b, c and d is a linear ordering such that a is most preferred and d is least preferred. Here $\{\{b\} : \beta, \{d\} : \beta \rightarrow \neg\alpha\}$ and $\{\{c\} : \neg\alpha\}$ are likely sources.

Assuming an ordering over development information is reasonable in software engineering. First, different kinds of information have different likelihoods of being incorrect. For example, method rules are unlikely to be incorrect, whereas some tentative specification information is quite possibly incorrect. Second, if a specification method is used interactively, a user can be asked to order pieces of specification according to likelihood of correctness.

10.6   Acting in the presence of inconsistency

The analysis described in the previous section can be used to generate a "report" that identifies inconsistencies and provides "diagnosis" of these inconsistencies. Using this, we should be able to identify possible actions that can be performed, based on the nature of the inconsistencies identified.

Acting in the presence of inconsistencies requires meta-level handling rules. This approach uses an action-based temporal logic that allows us to specify the past context and source of an inconsistency in order to prescribe future actions to handle the inconsistency [GH93a, FGH+94]. Thus for example the rule,

147

$$[data(\Delta_1) \wedge data(\Delta_2)$$
$$\wedge union(\Delta_1, \Delta_2) \vdash \bot$$
$$\wedge inconsistency\text{-}source(union(\Delta_1, \Delta_2), S)$$
$$\wedge likely\text{-}spelling\text{-}problem(S)$$
$$\wedge LAST^1 likely\text{-}spelling\text{-}problem(S)$$
$$\wedge LAST^2 likely\text{-}spelling\text{-}problem(S)]$$
$$\rightarrow NEXT^1 tell\text{-}user(\text{``is there a spell problem?''}, S)$$

specifies that the user should be prompted to check the inconsistent data for spelling mistakes. This rule uses the temporal operators $LAST^n$ and $NEXT^n$ to refer to n time units in the past or future, respectively. Also note that:

- $data(\Delta_1)$ and $data(\Delta_2)$ hold if the formulae in the databases Δ_1 and Δ_2, respectively, are logical rewrites of some development information.

- $union(\Delta_1, \Delta_2) \vdash \bot$ holds if the union of the databases Δ_1 and Δ_2 classically implies inconsistency.

- $inconsistency\text{-}source(union(\Delta_1, \Delta_2), S)$ holds if S is a minimally inconsistent subset of the union of Δ_1 and Δ_2, as defined in Section 10.5.1. The likely source, S, of the inconsistency may be identified, for example, as described in Section 10.5.2.

- $likely\text{-}spelling\text{-}problem(S)$ holds if the cause of the inconsistency is likely to result from typographical errors in S. Since we are using a temporal language at the meta-level, we can also include as conditions in our rule the fact that we haven't checked this problem at previous points S in time. In this way, the past history can affect future actions.

- $tell\text{-}user(\text{``is there a spell problem?''}, S)$ is an action that may be triggered if the inconsistency is identified as above. In this case, the action is a message displayed to the user, together with the likely source of the inconsistency.

Identifying the appropriate inconsistency handling action in a rule such as the one described above remains a difficult, but important, challenge. It depends on the kinds of inconsistency that can be detected and the degree of inconsistency tolerance that can be supported. Possible actions include the following [Nus96]:

Ignoring the inconsistency completely and continuing development regardless. This may be appropriate in certain circumstances where the inconsistency is isolated and does not prevent further development from taking place.

Circumventing the inconsistent parts of the specification being developed and continuing development. This may be appropriate in order to avoid inconsistent portions of the specification and/or to delay resolution of the inconsistency.

Removing the inconsistency altogether by correcting any mistakes or resolving conflicts. This depends on a clear identification of the inconsistency and assumes that the actions required to fix it are known. Restoring consistency completely can be difficult to achieve, and is quite often impossible to automate completely without human intervention.

Ameliorating inconsistent situations by performing actions that "improve" these situations and increase the possibility of future resolution. This is an attractive approach in situations where complete and immediate resolution is not possible (perhaps because further information is required from another development participant), but where some steps can be taken to "fix" part or some of the inconsistent information. This approach requires techniques for analysis and reasoning in the presence of inconsistency, such as those described in this paper.

Deciding which kind of action is appropriate or feasible to perform in the presence of inconsistency is the first step towards specifying effective inconsistency handling rules.

10.7 Automated reasoning and tool support

There are three broad areas of inconsistency management that are amenable to automated support. The first is in the area of inconsistency detection (see for example [Lin88]).

The second area is that of inconsistency classification. Here, the emphasis is on identifying the kind of inconsistency that has been detected in, or between, partial specifications. Tool support for this kind of activity is more limited, because there is little work that attempts to classify inconsistencies. Some tools (for example CONMAN [SK88]) search for one of a pre-defined number of kinds of inconsistency, and try to match the detected inconsistency with one of these.

The third area is that of inconsistency handling, which offers varied and challenging scope for tool support. For example, debuggers and negotiation-support tools can be used to facilitate removing inconsistencies and resolving conflicts. However, there are few tools available yet that explicitly support reasoning and analysis in the manner we have described here.

10.8   Prospects in systems engineering

The overwhelming majority of work on consistency management in systems engineering has dealt with tools and techniques for maintaining consistency and avoiding inconsistency. Increasingly, however, researchers have begun to study the notion of inconsistency in software systems, and have recognized the need to formalize this notion.

Whilst work on explicitly analysing inconsistent specifications in the manner described here is limited, a number of researchers have recognized the need to (1) tolerate inconsistency in software development, and (2) provide ways of acting in the presence of inconsistency.

In this chapter, we have explored the use of a logic-based approach to reasoning in the presence of inconsistency. We have seen how partial specifications might be translated into classical logic in order to detect inconsistencies between them. To overcome the trivialization of classical logic that results when an inconsistency is detected, we have considered the use of a paraconsistent logic which allows continued development in the presence of inconsistency.

We have also examined the use of a labelled language to "audit" reasoning results and to "diagnose" inconsistencies. The labels facilitated the identification of likely sources of inconsistencies. Such logical analysis also provided us with guidance about the actions one can perform in the presence of particular inconsistencies (for example, actions to resolve a conflict, delay resolution, ameliorate an inconsistent specification, etc.).

Chapter 11

Outlook for Uncertainty in Information Systems

11.1 Introduction

In this text, we have motivated the need to handle uncertain information, presented some formal approaches, and considered some applications. In this chapter, we conclude this coverage by considering the outlook for uncertainty in information systems, focusing on formalisms for uncertainty, and strategies for uncertainty.

11.2 Formalisms for uncertainty

We have stressed the importance of formal approaches for uncertainty in information systems. This is partly to support appropriate formal analysis of information systems and so minimize some risks involved in developing information systems. But, it is also to allow for a modular approach to developing systems. If we want to build large complex systems, then the ability to build them in a modular fashion has obvious benefits. To do this we need well-understood components. Relational databases are a good example of this. Building large databases from small components, namely relations, using relational algebra, or relational calculus, has delivered numerous advantages.

The emphasis of this text has been to provide a "feel" for the problems and possible solutions for handling uncertainty in information systems rather than on providing a very comprehensive and technical coverage of the area.

Hence, there are important formal approaches that we have chosen not to cover here including Dempster-Shafer theory [Sha76], an approach to reasoning with evidence, chaos theory (see for example [Hal92]), for modelling non-linear systems, genetic algorithms (see for example [Gol89]), also for modelling non-linear systems, and belief revision theory [Gar88], for handling inconsistencies between a database and an update. Also of interest are epistemic logics that are for reasoning with knowledge and beliefs (see for example [MvdH95]) and are of particular relevance for modelling agents. In addition, there is a lot of other relevant work on technologies and techniques for uncertainty in databases that we do not cover here including consistency checking in databases and updates in databases.

The mix of approaches here was chosen to represent a range of possibilities. Some of the formalisms are already being used in successful applications whilst others will not be used for some time. However, to draw an analogy with database technology, the role of formalisms for uncertainty are comparable with that of relational algebra. For these formalisms, there is now the opportunity to develop implementations, tools, querying techniques, and updating techniques, to give us the equivalent of relational database mangement systems.

We have also outlined the need for systems for uncertain information that have many capabilities that will only be realizable within artificial intelligence in the long term. Nevertheless, formal specification of such requirements can provide important goals for future developments.

11.3   Strategies for uncertainty

Clearly, improved use of uncertain information will become an increasingly important issue for organizations. The heterogeneous and complex nature of uncertainty means that handling it is challenging. To address this, organizations will have to incorporate computer-based handling of uncertain information into their information management strategies. This will become vital for the so-called "knowledge" companies.

In the short term this will focus on niche applications where some organizational advantage can be predicted with our current understanding. There is now a range of useful formalisms that can be used within the context of appropriate management strategies to provide profitable advanced information systems. These are systems with well-understood behaviours and with reasoning that is clearly explained and justified. However, as the advantages gained through systematic improvements in handling uncertain information become more numerous, the management of uncertainty will, in time, become a central theme in most information technology strategies.

Being cognizant of the heterogeneity of uncertain information will be important. Clearly harnessing probability theory and statistics is only part of the story. Management strategies must take a broader view. This includes attempting to capture qualitatively uncertain information that may be fuzzy, default, or inconsistent, and attempting to develop means to harness and aggregate hetrogeneous forms of uncertain information.

If an organization ignores uncertain information it will be operating at a disadvantage. Ignoring object-level information means that useful operational and strategic information will be unavailable. The ramifications will be diverse, but it will mean that members of the organization will not have access to information that could improve their decisions or processes.

Ignoring meta-level information means that members of the organization will not have adequate control over object-level information. Again the ramifications are diverse, but examples of problems include decision-makers not receiving the best information from the company information service, information disseminated over email not reaching the most appropriate groups, and work-group systems not optimizing the interaction between members.

Within management strategies, consideration also needs to be given to issues such as to the means and cost of acquiring and maintaining uncertain information. This may include consideration of issues of knowledge engineering, and of machine learning technology. Data mining, as discussed in Chapter 8, is also important for this goal.

In addition, consideration needs to be given to the risk of delegating the handling of uncertain information to computer-based systems. Some tasks are relatively risk-free. For example, instead of ordering incoming emails chronologically, a softbot could order them according to some default information that it has about the users' interests. In contrast, some tasks are clearly risky, such as foreign exchange or bond trading decisions. A management strategy should therefore include some form of risk-analysis, and perhaps for certain applications such as some decision-support tasks, adopt some form of quantitative or qualitative decision-theoretic reasoning facility, to qualify inferences.

At a more general level, harnessing uncertain information is part of a general trend towards intelligent organizations. Organizations can no longer operate by brute force. In this age of vicissitudes, organizations need to be more responsive, creative and knowledgeable. They need to think, collaborate and communicate with increasing ability. In essence, they need to be more intelligent.

An organization incorporates people who undertake intelligent activities, within and outside the organization. These activities include communicating, observing, investigating, learning, collaborating, adapting, and in particular decision making [But91]. An intelligent organization supports these activities by better information and better use of information. Computers will be the vehicles for delivering better information and the tools for better usage of the information. Clearly, uncertain information — both object-level and meta-level — is critically important in this trend.

Glossary

Abduction Process by which given some assumptions and a formula, where the assumptions do not imply the formula, further assumptions are identified such that when added to the original assumptions do imply the formula. For example, suppose we have the assumption "If the battery is flat, then the car will not start", and the observation "The car will not start", by abduction we can obtain the assumption "The battery is flat".

Ambiguous statement A statement that has more than one meaning. For example, "This food is hot" could mean that the temperature of the food is hot or that the food is spicy.

Argument A set of assumptions, together with a derivation of one or more inferences.

Argumentation Process by which arguments are constructed and compared.

Assumptions Information used for generating inferences.

Autoepistemic logic A type of non-monotonic logic.

Automated theorem proving Process by which theorems can be automatically derived from information according to the proof theory of some logic. An automated theorem proving program can be viewed as an inference engine.

Axiom Either (1) a property of a formal system, or (2) information that is certain.

Backward chaining reasoning In a rule-based system, a goal is satisfied if the goal is an assumption or if there is rule with the goal as consequent, and the conditions of the rule are satisfied. The conditions are therefore new goals. Synonymous with goal-directed reasoning. *See also* Forward-chaining reasoning.

Bayesian network A type of knowledge representation based on a directed graph where nodes represent random variables and causal relationships between these variables are represented by directed arcs in the graph.

Belief revision Process by which the set of beliefs derived from some information are revised when that information is updated.

Bias A systematic error in information.

Case-based system Information systems that use "cases" to represent information. For example, a decision-support system for advising on insolvency might have cases of insolvency as cases. For this approach to decision support, the user is usually interested in locating cases of interest. This is done by delineating the type of case that is of interest, often by keyword.

Closed-world assumption For some information, any information that is not implied is assumed to be false. For example, in an airline database, air routes are explicitly represented. If no route is represented for a pair of cities, then the assumption allows the inference that no route exists to be derived.

Conditional probability The probability that an event occurs given that another event has occurred.

Consequence Synonymous with inference.

Consistent information Information is consistent if there are no conflicts. When using a logic, information is consistent if and only if an inference and the negation of that inference cannot be derived.

Data Either (1) synonymous with information or (2) facts as opposed to more general knowledge.

Database A repository of information, usually with some organization, or structure, such as tables of data.

Database management system A software system for managing databases. Usually providing facilities for setting up, organizing, updating and querying a database.

Database system An information system composed of a database and a database management system.

Data completion Process by which missing data is substituted by data that is likely to be true. The substituted data is default information.

Data-driven reasoning Synonymous with forward chaining reasoning.

Data fusion Process of handling, and usually combining, information from heterogeneous sources. The need to combine information from multiple sources arises in diverse applications including: (1) fusing information from sensors, where imperfect measurements are taken and need to be aggregated; (2) fusing information from multiple databases, where information may be conflicting; and (3) fusing multiple expert opinions.

Data mining Process by which new knowledge is identified from repositories of information. It is a form of machine learning. Usually the repositories are large and the process looks for interesting relationships in the data. For example, a retail chain might notice that if two products are co-located, they sell more of both products.

Decidable A logic is decidable if and only if from any set of formulae and a formula of the language, the proof theory can ascertain in a finite number of steps whether or not the formula is an inference from the set of formulae. Classical propositional logic is decidable, though classical predicate logic is not.

Decision-support system An information system that assists an end-user in decision-making. Assistance could include provision of relevant information, reasoning with that information to make arguments for good decisions, and identifying qualifications or ramifications of possible decisions.

Deduction Process by which inferences are derived from some assumptions. Each step in a deduction is a logically valid step. Synonymous with derivation. *See also* Theorem proving.

Deductive database Synonymous with inferential database.

Declarative programming Type of programming where declarative statements such as logical statements or algebraic statements are used as programs. Programs are used by reasoning with these statements. *See also* Logic programming and Procedural programming.

157

Defeasible logic Synomymous with non-monotonic logic.

Default logic A type of non-monotonic logic.

Default rule Generally, it is of the form "If α holds, then β holds". Specifically, it is part of the language of default logic.

Default information Useful information that is usually true, though does have some exceptions. Often it is intuitive and advantageous to resort to defaults and therefore allow the inference of useful conclusions, even if it does entail making some mistakes as not all exceptions to these defaults are necessarily known. Default information includes heuristics, hypotheses, rules of conjecture, null values in data, closed-world assumptions for databases, and some qualitative abstractions of probabilistic information. Defaults are a natural and very common form of information. There are also obvious advantages to applying the same default a number of times. There is an economy in stating (and dealing with) only a general proposition instead of stating (and dealing with) maybe thousands of instances of such a general proposition.

Derivation Synonymous with deduction.

Erroneous information Synonymous with incorrect information.

Evidence Information about a situation or scenario that is either (1) used to establish an opinion, or (2) used as assumptions, maybe with some degree of uncertainty, for reasoning.

Expert system A type of knowledge-based system that emulates the problem solving behaviour of an expert in a restricted domain.

Facts Either (1) synonymous with information; (2) information that is certain; or (3) information that is specific to a given context. For the third case, consider a doctor advising a patient. Facts are information on a given patient, such as name, age, and blood pressure. This information is only applicable to that patient. This contrasts with information, often called knowledge, that can be used on all patients, such as "If a patient has high blood pressure and is middle-aged, then prescribe a low sodium diet".

Focus of information The degree of detail in information.

Formal language Type of language where every part of the language is fully and clearly defined. For example, the language of classical logic is a formal language.

Formal semantics Type of semantics where each part of the semantics is fully and clearly defined. For example, the semantics for classical logic is a formal semantics.

Formula A logical statement.

Forward chaining reasoning In a rule-based system, inferences are generated from the data and rules. The inferences are added to the data, and the process repeated. This can be repeated until a goal has been derived, or until no more inferences can be generated. Synonymous with data-driven reasoning. *See also* Backward chaining reasoning.

Fuzzy information Information that is vague or not precisely delineated. For example, "tall men", "fast cars", or "high salaries".

Fuzzy logic Generalization of classical logic. This includes fuzzy predicates and fuzzy truth values.

Fuzzy set theory Generalization of classical set theory. Notion of a set is generalized with degrees of membership. So for example, a Ferrari has a higher degree of membership of the set of fast cars than a Volvo.

Goal-directed reasoning Synonymous with backward chaining reasoning.

Heuristic A useful general rule, or principle, that is usually correct, though has some exceptions. Not all exceptions are necessarily known for the heuristic to be useful.

Hypothesis Information used to explain some observation or evidence. *See also* abduction and induction.

Inaccurate Significantly uncertain. Synonym for imprecise and inexact.

Induction Process by which more general information is generated from examples. For example, if a doctor observes that the majority of patients with disorder A treated with drug B are cured, then drug B is a good treatment for A.

Inexact Significantly uncertain. Synonym for inaccurate and imprecise.

159

Inference Information implied by other information.

Inference engine A program that automates the generation of inferences from information according to the definition for reasoning.

Inferential database A relational database that also contains rules. Inferences, in the form of further relations, can be derived using the relational data together with the rules. Synonymous with deductive database.

Information filtering Process by which information is filtered from an online source, such as emails, newsfeeds, etc. The aim is to help a user locate the more important or relevant information from the source. Often there is too much information coming in for the user to read it all and/or it would take the user too long to classify it all according to important or relevancy. A common means for facilitating information retrieval is for the user to delineate topics of interest or importance by keywords. Hence, information filtering is closely related to information retrieval.

Information retrieval Process by which information is retrieved from a repository. The aim is to provide a user with the "best possible" information from a database. The problem of information retrieval is determining what constitutes the best possible information for a given user. A common form of interaction for information retrieval is for the user to offer a set of keywords. These are then used by the information retrieval system to identify information that meets the user's needs. For example, in a bibliographic database, a user might be interested in finding papers on some topic. The keywords would be an attempt to delineate that topic, and so used to improve precision (ensuring that a significant proportion of the items retrieved are relevant to the user) and recall (ensuring that a significant proportion of the relevant items are retrieved).

Imprecise Significantly uncertain. Synonym for inaccurate and inexact.

Knowledge Either (1) synonynous with information or (2) information that is reusable. For the latter, consider a doctor advising a patient. Knowledge would be information such as "If a patient has high blood pressure and is middle-aged, then prescribe a low sodium diet". This information can be used on all patients, whereas information on a given patient, such as name, age, and blood pressure, is only applicable to that patient. This second kind of information is often called a set of facts.

Knowledge-base A repository of knowledge, usually with some organization or structure such as production rules, logical statements, semantic networks, or Bayesian networks.

Knowledge-based system A program that incorporates knowledge represented in some explicit form, a knowledge-base, and an inference engine that allows conclusions to be drawn from that knowledge. *See also* Expert system.

Knowledge discovery Synonymous with data mining.

Knowledge representation Method for representing knowledge in a formalism that supports inferencing.

Logic A logic is a formal language for statements, or propositions, together with proof rules, to manipulate sets of statements.

Logic programming A form of computer programming where the program is a set of statements in some logic (most logic programming languages are based on classical logic), and the program is used by asking logical queries. The execution of the program is defined by the proof theory of the logic. Hence, it can be viewed as automated theorem proving. It is a form of declarative programming.

Machine learning Process for generating new knowledge from information.

Meta-level uncertainty In order for an information system to handle object-level information, there is a need for extra information about the object-level information, and about the possible users of that information. Whilst meta-level information is used to facilitate the information system meeting the end-user's needs, it is not actually seen, or used directly, by the end-user. For instance meta-level information can be used to increase or decrease the amount of information given in answer to a query, whereas the answer is actually object-level information.

Monotonic reasoning Reasoning is monotonic if the set of inferences increases when the set of assumptions increases.

Non-monotonic logic A logic is non-monotonic if it permits non-monotonic reasoning.

Non-monotonic reasoning Reasoning is non-monotonic if it is not monotonic. Reasoning with default information is non-monotonic since when extra assumptions are used, inferences might need to be retracted. This is because extra assumptions can mean the exceptions to default information apply, and the default inferences need to be retracted.

Negation-as-failure A type of negation. If a formula α cannot be inferred from some assumptions, then the assumptions imply $\sim \alpha$, where $\sim$ denotes negation-as-failure.

Object-level information Within an organization, the purpose of an information system is to handle information for some benefit to the organization. Object-level information is that which an end-user is using. The user is aware of the existence of object-level information in the system. Queries to, and answers from, the system are in terms of the object-level information.

Open-world assumption For some information, any inference that is not implied is not assumed to be false. *See also* Closed world assumption.

Possibility theory Theory for modelling the notion of possibility.

Possibilistic logic A logic where propositions are true or false, but due to lack of precision of the available information, there is only an estimate of the possibility or necessity that a given proposition is true. *See also* Fuzzy logic.

Probability theory A set of axioms that captures the intuitive notion of probability.

Procedural programming Type of programming where programs are sets of instructions. *See also* declarative programming.

Production rules A type of knowledge representation. Rules are of the form "If $condition_1$ holds and ... and $condition_n$ holds then *consequent* holds".

Proof rule Definition of the ways that logical statements can be manipulated in a logic. These manipulations are derivations, and result in inferences.

Proof theory Definition of the ways that logical statements can be manipulated in a logic. These manipulations give inferences.

Proposition A logical statement.

Reasoning Process by which information is analysed, and may include one or more of deduction, abduction, and induction.

Rebutting argument An argument that rebuts another argument. If an argument is of the form β holds, a rebutting argument takes the position that $\neg\beta$ holds, hence rebutting the argument for β. *See also* Undercutting argument.

Relational database A database where all the object-level information is in the form of relations, or equivalently tables. For example, for a staff database, the form of the relation might be *staff(name,age,job,salary)*.

Rule-based system A type of knowledge-based system where the knowledge is in the form of production rules.

Semantics The meaning of a language or system. For example, in classical logic, semantics are based on formulae being either true or false. The meaning of complex formulae are then defined in terms of the meaning of simpler formulae. For example, if α is true and β is true, then $\alpha \wedge \beta$ is true.

Semantic network A type of knowledge representation. The nodes of a semantic network represent objects, and the links represent relationships. For example, "bird" and "animal" could be nodes, and relationship "is-a" holds between bird and animal.

Semi-decidable A logic is semi-decidable if and only if when a formula is a consequence of a set of formulae, then the proof theory can be used to construct a proof in a finite number of steps. Classical predicate logic is semi-decidable.

Tautology A logical statement that is always true for a logic. For example, for classical logic, $\alpha \vee \neg\alpha$ is a tautology. Note classical logic has many tautologies.

Textual information Information in the form of written words or sentences of natural language.

Theory A set of logical statements, usually modelling some concepts, systems or phenomena.

Theorem Either (1) a general property of a formal system that can be proved mathematically or (2) a logical inference from a set of logical statements.

Theorem proving Process of generating theorems. *See also* Deduction.

Tolerance Permissible degree of uncertainty in information.

Undercutting argument An argument that undercuts another argument. If an argument is of the form "If α holds and α usually implies β, therefore β holds", a undercutting argument takes the position that $\neg\alpha$ holds, hence undercutting the argument for β. *See also* Rebutting argument.

Unknown Information that cannot be derived from known information.

Unpredictable Difficult to infer, from known information, the likely outcome of a future event.

Vague information Information that is not clearly defined or delineated.

Bibliography

[ABM94]   R Almond, J Bradshaw, and D Madigan. Revise and sharing
            of graphical belief network components. In P Cheeseman and
            W Oldford, editors, *Selecting Models from Data*, pages 113–122.
            Springer, 1994.

[AC91]   W Atkinson and J Cunningham. Proving properties of safety-
            critical systems. *IEE Software Engineering Journal*, 6(2):41–50,
            1991.

[And89]   B Andrews. *Successful Expert Systems: Twenty-four studies of
            British organizations with expert systems in successful opera-
            tion*. Financial Times Business Information, 1989.

[AOJJ89]   S Andersen, K Olesen, F V Jensen, and F Jensen. Hugin – a
            shell for building bayesian belief universes for expert systems. In
            *Proceedings of the Tenth International Joint Conference on Ar-
            tificial Intelligence*, pages 1080–1085. Morgan Kaufmann, 1989.

[AWFA87]   S Andreassen, M Woldbye, B Falck, and S Andersen. MUNIN –
            a causal probabilistic network for interpretation of electromyo-
            graphic findings. In *Proceedings of the Tenth International
            Joint Conference on Artificial Intelligence (IJCAI'87)*, pages
            366–372, 1987.

[Bac90]   F Bacchus. *Representing and Reasoning with Probabilisitic
            Knowledge: A Logical Approach to Probabilities*. MIT Press,
            1990.

[Bal87]   J Baldwin. Evidential support logic programming. *Fuzzy Sets
            and Systems*, 24:1–26, 1987.

[Bal91]   R Balzer. Tolerating inconsistency. In *proceedings of the 13th International Conference on Software Engineering*, pages 158–165. IEEE Press, 1991.

[BC92]   N Belkin and B Croft. Information filtering and information retrieval: Two sides of the same coin. *Communications of the ACM*, 35:29–38, 1992.

[BCD+93]   S Benferhat, C Cayrol, D Dubois, J Lang, and H Prade. Inconsistency management and prioritized syntax-based entailment. In *Proceedings of the Thirteenth International Joint Conference on Artificial Intelligence*, pages 640–645. Morgan Kaufmann, 1993.

[BdCGH95]   Ph Besnard, L Farinas del Cerro, D Gabbay, and A Hunter. Logical handling of default and inconsistent information. In Ph Smets and A Motro, editors, *Uncertainty Management in Information Systems*. Kluwer, 1995.

[Bel77]   N Belnap. A useful four-valued logic. In G Epstein, editor, *Modern Uses of Multiple-valued Logic*, pages 8–37. Reidel, 1977.

[Bes89]   Ph Besnard. *An Introduction to Default Logic*. Springer, 1989.

[Bes91]   Ph Besnard. Paraconsistent logic approach to knowledge representation. In M de Glas M and D Gabbay D, editors, *Proceedings of the First World Conference on Fundamentals of Artificial Intelligence*, pages 107–114. Angkor, 1991.

[BG88a]   J Boose and B Gaines. *Knowledge Acquisition Tools for Expert Systems: Volume 1*. Academic Press, 1988.

[BG88b]   J Boose and B Gaines. *Knowledge Acquisition Tools for Expert Systems: Volume 2*. Academic Press, 1988.

[BGH88]   P Bosc, M Galibourg, and G Hemon. Fuzzy querying with sql: Extensions and implementation aspects. *Fuzzy Sets and Systems*, 28:333–349, 1988.

[BGMP92]   D Barbara, H Garcia-Molina, and D Porter. The management of probabilistic data. *IEEE Transactions on Knowledge and Data Engineering*, 4:487–502, 1992.

[BH94]   P Bruza and T Huibers. Investigating aboutness axioms using information fields. In *Proceedings of the Eighteenth ACM SI-GIR Conference on Research and Development in Information Retrieval (SIGIR'94)*, pages 112–121. Springer, 1994.

[BH95]   Ph Besnard and A Hunter. Quasi-classical logic: Non-trivializable classical reasoning from inconsistent information. In C Froidevaux and J Kohlas, editors, *Symbolic and Quantitative Approaches to Uncertainty*, Lecture Notes in Computer Science, pages 44–51, 1995.

[Bib93]   W Bibel. *Deduction: Automated logic.* Academic Press, 1993.

[BK95]   P Bosc and J Kacprzyk, editors. *Fuzziness in Database Management Systems.* Physica Verlag, 1995.

[BP95]   P Bosc and H Prade. An introduction to fuzzy set and possibility theory-based approaches to the treatment of uncertainty and imprecision in database management systems. In Ph Smets and A Motro, editors, *Uncertainty Management in Information Systems*. Kluwer, 1995.

[Bre89]   G Brewka. Preferred subtheories: an extended logical framework for default reasoning. In *Proceedings of the Eleventh International Joint Conference on Artificial Intelligence (IJCAI'89)*, pages 1043–1048, 1989.

[Bre91]   G Brewka. *Common-sense Reasoning.* Cambridge University Press, 1991.

[Bre94]   G Brewka. Reasoning about priorities in default logic. In *Proceedings of the Twelfth National Conference on Artificial Intelligence (AAAI'94)*, pages 940–954. MIT Press, 1994.

[BS94]   S Brüning and T Schaub. Using classical theorem-proving techniques for approximate reasoning. In B Bouchon-Meunier and R Yager, editors, *Proceedings of the Fifth International Conference on Information Processing and Management of Uncertainty in Knowledge-based Systems*, pages 493–498. IPMU, 1994.

[Bun95]   W Buntine. A guide to the literature on learning probabilistic networks from data. *IEEE Transactions on Knowledge and Data Engineering*, 1995. Submitted.

[But91]   R Butler. *Designing Organizations: A Decision Making Perspective*. Routledge, 1991.

[BZ84]   J Baldwin and Q Zhou. A fuzzy relational inference engine. *Fuzzy Sets and Systems*, 14:155–174, 1984.

[CA91]   E Castillo and E Alvarez. *Expert Systems: Uncertainty and Learning*. Computational Mechanics Publications and Elsevier Applied Science, 1991.

[CC92]   Y Chiamaramella and J Chevallet. About retrieval models and logic. *The Computer Journal*, 35:233–242, 1992.

[CCB90]   M Costa, R Cunningham, and J Booth. Logical animation. In *Proceedings of the Twelfth International conference on software engineering*, pages 144–149. IEEE Computer Society Press, 1990.

[CEG94]   M Cadoli, T Eiter, and G Gottlob. Default logic as a query language. In J Doyle, E Sandewall, and P Torasso, editors, *Principles of Knowledge Representation and Reasoning: Proceedings of the Fourth International Conference*, pages 99–108. Morgan Kaufmann, 1994.

[Cha91]   E Charniak. Bayesian networks without tears. *AI Magazine*, 12:50–63, 1991.

[Che86]   P Cheeseman. Probabilistic versus fuzzy reasoning. In L Kanal and J Lemmer, editors, *Uncertainty in Artificial Intelligence*, pages 85–102. Elsevier, 1986.

[Cho94]   L Cholvy. A logical approach to multi-source reasoning. In *Proceedings of the Applied Logic Conference*, volume 808 of *Lecture Notes in Computer Science*, pages 183–196. Springer, 1994.

[CHS93]   J Cussens, A Hunter, and A Srinivasan. Generating explicit orderings for non-monotonic logics. In *Proceedings of the Eleventh National Conference on Artificial Intelligence (AAAI'93)*, pages 420–425. MIT Press, 1993.

[Cla90]   D Clark. Numerical and symbolic approaches to uncertainty management in artificial intelligence. *Artificial Intelligence Review*, 4:109–146, 1990.

[Cod86]   E Codd. Missing information in relation databases. *ACM SIGMOD*, 15, 1986.

[Coo84]   G Cooper. Nestor: A computer-based medical diagnostic that integrates causal and probabilistic knowledge. Technical Report HPP-84-48, Stanford University, 1984.

[Coo90]   G Cooper. Computational complexity of probabilistic inference using bayesian networks. *Artificial Intelligence*, 42:393–405, 1990.

[Cro93]   B Croft. Knowledge-based and statistical approaches to text retrieval. *IEEE Expert*, pages 8–12, April 1993.

[D'A88]   A D'Agapeyeff. The nature of expertise and its elicitation for business expert systems: A commentary. *Knowledge Engineering Review*, 3:147–158, 1988.

[dC74]   N C da Costa. On the theory of inconsistent formal systems. *Notre Dame Journal of Formal Logic*, 15:497–510, 1974.

[DdC88]   R Demolombe and L Farinas del Cerro. An algebraic evaluation method for deduction in incomplete databases. *Journal of Logic Programming*, 5:183–205, 1988.

[Dem95]   R Demolombe. Uncertainty in intelligent databases. In Ph Smets and A Motro, editors, *Uncertainty Management in Information Systems: From Needs to Solutions*. Kluwer, 1995.

[Den86]   T Denvir. *Introduction to Discrete Mathematics for Software Engineering*. Macmillan, 1986.

[Die49]   Z Dienes. On an implication function in many-valued systems of logic. *Journal of Symbolic Logic*, 14:95–97, 1949.

[DLP94]   D Dubois, J Lang, and H Prade. Possibilistic logics. In D Gabbay, C Hogger, and J Robinson, editors, *Handbook of Logic in Artificial Intelligence and Computer Science, Volume 3, Nonmonotonic Reasoning and Uncertainty Reasoning*, pages 439–513. Oxford University Press, 1994.

[DNP94]   C Damasio, W Nejdl, and L Pereira. REVISE: An extended
            logic programming system for revising knowledge bases. In
            J Doyle, E Sandewall, and P Torasso, editors, *Principles of
            Knowledge Representation and Reasoning: Proceedings of the
            Fourth International Conference*, pages 607–618. Morgan Kauf-
            mann, 1994.

[Doy79]   J Doyle. A truth maintenance system. *Artificial Intelligence*,
            12:231–272, 1979.

[DP87]   D Dubois and H Prade. Necessity measures and the resolution
            principle. *IEEE Transactions on Systems, Man and Cybernet-
            ics*, 17:474–478, 1987.

[DP88a]   D Dubois and H Prade. An introduction to possibilistic and
            fuzzy logics. In Ph Smets, E Mamdani, D Dubois, and H Prade,
            editors, *Non-standard Logics for Automated Reasoning*. Aca-
            demic Press, 1988.

[DP88b]   D Dubois and H Prade. Processing of imprecision and uncer-
            tainty in expert system reasoning models. In C Ernst, edi-
            tor, *Management Expert Systems*, pages 67–88. Addison Wes-
            ley, 1988.

[DP94]   D Dubois and H Prade. Combination of fuzzy information in
            the framework of possibility theory. In M Abidi and R Gonza-
            lez, editors, *Data Fusion in Robotics and Machine Intelligence*,
            pages 481–505. Academic Press, 1994.

[DPY95]   D Dubois, H Prade, and R Yager, editors. *Readings in Fuzzy
            Sets for Intelligent Systems*. Morgan Kaufmann, 1995.

[EGH95]   M Elvang-Goransson and A Hunter. Argumentative logics:
            Reasoning from classically inconsistent information. *Data and
            Knowledge Engineering Journal*, 16:125–145, 1995.

[EN95]   S Easterbrook and B Nuseibeh. Managing inconsistencies in an
            evolving specification. In *Proceedings of Second International
            Symposium on Requirements Engineering (RE '95)*, pages 48–
            55. IEEE CS Press, 1995.

[FBY92]   W Frakes and R Baeza-Yates, editors. *Information Retrieval:
            Data Structures and Algorithms*. Prentice Hall, 1992.

[FdF95]   R Fung and B del Favero. Applying Bayesian networks to information retrieval. *Communications of the ACM*, 38:42–57, 1995.

[Feh93]   D Fehrer. A unifying framework for reason maintenance. In M Clarke, R Kruse, and S Moral, editors, *Symbolic and Qualitative Approaches to Reasoning and Uncertainty (EC-SQARU'93)*, volume 747 of *Lecture Notes in Computer Science*, pages 113–120. Springer, 1993.

[Fel68]   W Feller. *An Introduction to Probability Theory*. John Wiley, 1968.

[FGH+94]   A Finkelstein, D Gabbay, A Hunter, J Kramer, and B Nuseibeh. Inconsistency handling in multi-perspective specifications. *Transactions on Software Engineering*, 20(8):569–578, 1994.

[Fit90]   M Fitting. *First-order Logic and Automated Theorem Proving*. Springer, 1990.

[FKN+92]   A Finkelstein, J Kramer, B Nuseibeh, L Finkelstein, and M. Goedicke. Viewpoints: A framework for multiple perspectives in system development. *International Journal of Software Engineering and Knowledge Engineering, Special issue on Trends and Future Research Directions in SEE*, 2(1):31–57, 1992.

[Fla94]   P Flach. *Simply Logical: Intelligent Reasoning by Example*. John Wiley, 1994.

[FM84]   E Feigenbaum and P McCorduck. *The Fifth Generation*. Pan Books, 1984.

[Fox86]   J Fox. Three arguments for extending the framework of probability. In L Kanal and J Lemmer, editors, *Uncertainty in Artificial Intelligence*, pages 447–458. Elsevier, 1986.

[FPSM91]   W Frawley, G Piatetsky-Shapiro, and C Matheus. Knowledge-discovery in databases: An overview. In G Piatetsky-Shapiro and W Frawley, editors, *Knowledge-discovery in Databases*. MIT Press, 1991.

171

[FPSSU96]   U Fayyard, G Piatetsky-Shapiro, P Smyth, and R Uthurusamy. *Advances in Knowledge Discovery and Data Mining.* AAAI Press and MIT Press, 1996.

[FU95]   U Fayyard and R Uthurusamy. *Proceedings of the First International Conference of Knowledge Discovery and Data Mining.* AAAI Press and MIT Press, 1995.

[FUV83]   R Fagin, J Ullman, and M Vardi. On the semantics of updates in databases. In *Proceedings of the Second Annual Association of Computing Machinery Symposium on Principles of Database Systems,* pages 352 365. ACM Press, 1983.

[Fuz93]   *Proceedings of the Second IEEE International Conference on Fuzzy Systems.* IEEE Computer Society, 1993.

[Fuz94a]   A fuzzy logic symposium. *IEEE Expert,* 9:3–46, 1994.

[Fuz94b]   *Proceedings of the Third IEEE International Conference on Fuzzy Systems.* IEEE Computer Society, 1994.

[Gab93]   D Gabbay. Labelled deductive systems: A position paper. In J Oikkonen and J Vaananen, editors, *Proceedings of the Logic Colloquium'90,* volume 2 of *Lecture Notes on Logic,* pages 66–88. Springer, 1993.

[Gab96]   D Gabbay. *Labelled Deductive Systems.* Oxford University Press, 1996.

[Gar88]   P Gardenfors. *Knowledge in Flux.* MIT Press, 1988.

[GB90]   B Gaines and J Boose. *Machine Learning and Uncertain Reasoning.* Academic Press, 1990.

[GB91]   J Grzymala-Busse. *Managing Uncertainty in Expert Systems.* Kluwer, 1991.

[GC91]   R Goldman and E Charniak. Dynamic construction of belief networks. In P Bonissone, M Henrion, L Kanal, and J Lemmer, editors, *Uncertainty in Artificial Intelligence 6,* pages 171–184. Elsevier, 1991.

[GD95]   M Goldszmidt and A Darwiche. Plan simulation using bayesian networks. In *Proceedings of the Eleventh Conference on Artificial Intelligence for Applications*, pages 155–161. IEEE Computer Society Press, 1995.

[GH91]   D Gabbay and A Hunter. Making inconsistency respectable 1: A position paper. In Ph Jorrand and J Keleman, editors, *Fundamentals of Artificial Intelligence Research*, volume 535 of *Lecture Notes in Artificial Intelligence*, pages 19–32. Springer, 1991.

[GH93a]   D Gabbay and A Hunter. Making inconsistency respectable 2: Meta-level handling of inconsistent data. In M Clarke, R Kruse, and S Moral, editors, *Symbolic and Qualitative Approaches to Reasoning and Uncertainty (ECSQARU'93)*, volume 747 of *Lecture Notes in Computer Science*, pages 129–136. Springer, 1993.

[GH93b]   D Gabbay and A Hunter. Restricted access logics for inconsistent information. In M Clarke, R Kruse, and S Moral, editors, *Symbolic and Qualitative Approaches to Reasoning and Uncertainty (ECSQARU'93)*, volume 747 of *Lecture Notes in Computer Science*, pages 137–144. Springer, 1993.

[GHR94]   D Gabbay, C Hogger, and J Robinson, editors. *Handbook of Logic in Artificial Intelligence and Logic Programming: Volume 3 – Non-monotonic Reasoning and Uncertainty Reasoning*. Oxford University Press, 1994.

[Gin87]   M Ginsberg. *Readings in Non-monotonic Reasoning*. Morgan Kaufmann, 1987.

[Gin91]   M Ginsberg. Knowledge interchange format: The KIF of death. *AI Magazine*, 12:57–63, 1991.

[GK95]   J Gebhardt and R Kruse. Learning possibilistic networks from data. In D Fisher and H Lenz, editors, *Artificial Intelligence and Statistics*, Lecture Notes in Statistics. Springer, 1995.

[GL90]   R Guha and D Lenat. CYC: A midterm report. *AI Magazine*, 11:32–59, 1990.

[GL93]   G Guardalben and D Lucarella. Information retrieval based on fuzzy reasoning. *Data and Knowledge Engineering*, 10:29–44, 1993.

[Gol89]   D Goldberg. *Genetic Algorithms in Search Optimization and Machine Learning*. Addison-Wesley, 1989.

[Hal90]   J Halpern. An analysis of first-order logics of probability. *Artificial Intelligence*, 46:311–350, 1990.

[Hal92]   N Hall. *The New Scientist Guide to Chaos*. Penguin, 1992.

[HBH91]   M Henrion, J Breese, and E Horvitz. Decision analysis and expert systems. *AI Magazine*, pages 64–91, 1991.

[Hec91a]   D Heckerman. *Probabilistic Similarity Networks*. MIT Press, 1991.

[Hec91b]   D Heckerman. Similarity networks for the construction of multiple-fault belief networks. In P Bonissone, M Henrion, L Kanal, and J Lemmer, editors, *Uncertainty in Artificial Intelligence 6*, pages 51–64. Elsevier, 1991.

[Hen89]   M Henrion. Some practical issues in constructing belief networks. In L Kanal, T Levitt, and J Lemmer, editors, *Uncertainty in Artificial Intelligence 3*. Elsevier, 1989.

[Hen95]   M Henrion. Probabilistic and Bayesian representation of uncertainty in information systems: A pragmatic approach. In Ph Smets and A Motro, editors, *Uncertainty Management in Information Systems*. Kluwer, 1995.

[HH88]   D Heckerman and E Horvitz. The myth of modularity in rule-based systems for reasoning with uncertainty. In J Lemmer and L Kanal, editors, *Uncertainty in Artificial Intelligence 2*, pages 23–34. Elsevier, 1988.

[HN96]   A Hunter and B Nuseibeh. Managing inconsistent specifications: Analysis, reasoning and actions. Technical report, Imperial College, 1996.

[HO82]   L Holmblad and J Ostergaard. Control of a cement kiln by fuzzy logic. In M Gupta and E Sanchez, editors, *Fuzzy Information and Decision Processes*, pages 389–400. North-Holland, 1982.

[Hod77]   W Hodges. *Logic: An Introduction to Elementary Logic.* Penguin, 1977.

[Hol89]   S Holtzman. *Intelligent Decision Systems.* Addison Wesley, 1989.

[Hop93]   M Hopkins. Default logic: Orderings and extensions. In *Symbolic and Qualitative Approaches to Reasoning and Uncertainty*, volume 747 of *Lecture Notes in Computer Science*, pages 174–179. Springer, 1993.

[Hun95]   A Hunter. Using default logic in information retrieval. In C Froidevaux and J Kohlas, editors, *Symbolic and Quantitative Approaches to Reasoning and Uncertainty*, volume 946 of *Lecture Notes in Computer Science*, pages 235–242, 1995.

[HW95]   D Heckerman and M Wellman. Bayesian networks. *Communications of the ACM*, 38:27–30, 1995.

[JHGJ88]   T Johnson, J Hewett, C Guilfoyle, and J Jeffcoate. *Expert Systems Markets and Suppliers.* Ovum, 1988.

[JK90]   U. Junker and K. Konolige. Computing the extensions of autoepistemic and default logics with a truth maintenance system. In *Proceedings of the Eighth National Conference on Artifical Intelligence (AAAI'90)*, pages 278–283. MIT Press, 1990.

[KAEGF95]   P Krause, S Ambler, M Elvang-Goransson, and J Fox. A logic of argumentation for reasoning under uncertainty. *Computational Intelligence*, 11:113–131, 1995.

[KC93]   P Krause and D Clark. *Representing Uncertain Knowledge: An Artificial Intelligence Approach.* Intellect, 1993.

[Ker90]   R Kerry. *Integrating Knowledge-based and Database Management Systems.* Ellis Horwood, 1990.

[KGK94]   R Kruse, J Gebhardt, and F Klawonn. *Foundations of Fuzzy Systems.* J Wiley, 1994.

[Kle86]   J De Kleer. An assumption-based TMS. *Artificial Intelligence*, 28:127–162, 1986.

[Kol91]   J Kolodner. Improving human decision making through case-based decision aiding. *AI Magazine*, 12:52–68, 1991.

[Kol94]   J Kolodner. *Case-based Reasoning*. Morgan Kaufmann, 1994.

[Kro93]   R Krovetz. Viewing morphology as an inference process. In R Koffhage, E Rasmussen, and P Willet, editors, *Proceedings of the Sixteenth ACM SIGIR Conference on Research and Development in Information Retrieval (SIGIR'93)*, pages 191–202. ACM Press, 1993.

[Lee92]   S Lee. An extended relational database model for uncertain and imprecise information. In *Proceedings of the 18th Conference on Very Large Databases*. Morgan Kaufmann, 1992.

[LG90]   D Lenat and R Guha. *Building Large Knowledge-based Systems*. Addison-Wesley, 1990.

[Lin87]   D Lindley. The probability approach to the treatment of uncertainty in artificial intelligence and expert systems. *Statistical Science*, 2:3–44, 1987.

[Lin88]   P A Lindsay. A survey of mechanical support for formal reasoning. *Software Engineering Journal (special issue on mechanical support for formal reasoning)*, 3:3–27, 1988.

[Lip65]   S Lipschutz. *Theory and Problems of Probability*. McGraw-Hill, 1965.

[Liu85]   C Liu. *Elements of Discrete Mathematics*. McGraw–Hill, 1985.

[LL90]   D Li and D Liu. *A Fuzzy Prolog Database System*. Research Studies Press, 1990.

[Lou87]   R Loui. Defeat among arguments: A system of defeasible inference. *Computational Intelligence*, 3:100–106, 1987.

[LS88]   S Lauritzen and D Siegelhalter. Local computations with probabilities on graphical structures and their application to expert systems. *Journal of the Royal Statistical Society B*, 50:157–224, 1988.

[LS95]   T Linke and T Schaub. Lemma handling in default logic theo-
              rem provers. In C Froidevaux and J Kohlas, editors, *Symbolic
              and Qualitative Approaches to Reasoning and Uncertainty*, vol-
              ume 946 of *Lecture Notes in Computer Science*, pages 285–292.
              Springer, 1995.

[Luk67]   J Lukasiewicz. On three-valued logic. In S McCall, editor,
              Polish Logic. Oxford University Press, 1967.

[Mam76]   E Mamdani. Advances in linguistic synthesis of fuzzy con-
              trollers. *International Journal of Man Machine Studies*, 8:669–
              678, 1976.

[McC86]   J McCarthy. Applications of circumscription to formalizing
              common-sense knowledge. *Artificial Intelligence*, 28:89–116,
              1986.

[MH69]   J McCarthy and P Hayes. Some philosophical problems from
              the standpoint of artifical intelligence. In B Meltzer and
              D Michie, editors, *Machine Intelligence 4*. Edinburgh Univer-
              sity Press, 1969.

[MH96]   P McBrien and A Hunter. Software engineering for default
              knowledge in information systems. Technical report, Imperial
              College, 1996.

[MJ94]   T Munakata and Y Jani. Fuzzy systems: An overview. *Com-
              munications of the ACM*, 37(3):69–76, 1994.

[MMH$^+$76]   A Miller, W Merkhofer, R Howard, J Matheson, and T Rice.
              Development of automated aids for decision analysis. Technical
              report, Stanford Research Institute, Menlo Park, California,
              1976.

[Mot95]   A Motro. Sources of uncertainty in information systems. In
              Ph Smets and A Motro, editors, *Uncertainty Management in
              Information Systems*. Kluwer, 1995.

[MR92]   H Mannila and K-J Räihaä. *The Design of Relational
              Databases*. Addison-Wesley, 1992.

177

[MS75]   P Magrez and Ph Smets. Fuzzy modus ponens: A new model
            suitable for applications in knowledge-based systems. *Interna-
            tional Journal of Intelligent Systems*, 4:181–200, 1975.

[MS88]   J Martins and S Shapiro. A model of belief revision. *Artificial
            Intelligence*, 35:25–79, 1988.

[MSD89]   M Mukaidono, Z Shen, and L Ding. Fundamentals of fuzzy pro-
            log. *International Journal of Approximate Reasoning*, 3:179–
            193, 1989.

[MSST93]   C Meghini, F Sebastiani, U Straccia, and C Thanos. A model
            of information retrieval based on a terminological logic. In *Pro-
            ceedings of the 16th ACM SIGIR Conference on Research and
            Development in Information Retrieval (SIGIR'93)*, pages 298–
            307. ACM Press, 1993.

[MT93]   W. Marek and M Truszczyński. *Nonmonotonic Logic: Context-
            Dependent Reasoning*. Springer-Verlag, 1993.

[Mug92]   S Muggleton. *Inductive Logic Programming*. Academic Press,
            1992.

[MvdH95]   J-J Meyer and W van der Hoek. *Epistemic Logic for Artifi-
            cial Intelligence and Computer Science*. Cambridge University
            Press, 1995.

[Nea88]   I Neale. First generation expert systems: A review of knowl-
            edge acquisition methodologies. *Knowledge Engineering Re-
            view*, 3:105–145, 1988.

[Nea90]   E Neapolitan. *Probabilistic Reasoning in Expert Systems*. John
            Wiley, 1990.

[NFF$^+$91] R Neches, R Fikes, T Finin, T Gruber, R Patil, T Senator, and
            W Swartout. Enabling technologies for knowledge sharing. *AI
            Magazine*, 12:36–56, 1991.

[Nie92]   J-Y Nie. Towards a probabilistic modal logic for semantic-based
            information retrieval. In *Proceedings of the 15th ACM SIGIR
            Conference on Research and Development in Information Re-
            trieval (SIGIR'92)*, pages 140–151. ACM Press, 1992.

[Nie94]   I. Niemelä. A decision method for nonmonotonic reasoning based on autoepistemic reasoning. In J Doyle, E Sandewall, and P Torasso, editors, *Proceedings of the Fourth International Conference Principles of Knowledge Representation and Reasoning*, pages 473–484. Morgan Kaufmann, 1994.

[Nil86]   N Nilsson. Probabilistic logic. *Artificial Intelligence*, 28:71–87, 1986.

[NKF94]   B Nuseibeh, J Kramer, and A Finkelstein. A framework for expressing the relationships between multiple views in requirements specification. *Transactions on Software Engineering*, 20(10):760–773, 1994.

[Nor68]   D North. A tutorial introduction to decision theory. *IEEE Transactions on Systems Science and Cybernetics*, 4:200–210, 1968.

[NR90]   S Naqvi and F Rossi. Reasoning in inconsistent databases. In *Logic Programming: Proceedings of the North American Conference*. MIT Press, 1990.

[NR92]   I. Niemelä and J. Rintanen. On the impact of stratification on the complexity of nonmonotonic reasoning. In B Nebel and W Swartout, editors, *Principles of Knowledge Representation and Reasoning: Proceedings of the Third International Conference*, pages 627–638. Morgan Kaufmann, 1992.

[Nus96]   B Nuseibeh. To be and not to be: On managing inconsistency in software development. In *Proceedings of the Eighth International Workshop on Software Specification and design*. IEEE Computer Society Press, 1996.

[Nut87]   J Nutter. Uncertainty and probability. In *Proceedings of the International Joint Conference on Artificial Intelligence*, pages 373–379. Morgan Kaufmann, 1987.

[PAP94]   *Second International Conference on Practical Applications of Prolog*. Practical Applications, 1994.

[PAP95]   *Third International Conference on Practical Applications of Prolog*. Practical Applications, 1995.

179

[Par96]   S Parsons. Imperfect information and databases. *IEEE Knowledge and Data Engineering*, 1996. In press.

[Pea86]   J Pearl. Fusion, propagation and structuring belief networks. *Artificial Intelligence*, 29:241–288, 1986.

[Pea87]   J Pearl. Bayesian decision methods. In *Encyclopedia of Artificial Intelligence*, pages 48–56. John Wiley, 1987.

[Pea88]   J Pearl. *Probabilistic Reasoning in Intelligent Systems: Networks of plausible inference*. Morgan Kaufmann, 1988.

[Poo85]   D Poole. A logical framework for default reasoning. *Artificial Intelligence*, 36:27–47, 1985.

[Pra93]   H Prakken. An argumentation framework for default reasoning. *Annals of Mathematics and Artificial Intelligence*, 9, 1993.

[RBP+91]   J Rumbaugh, M Blaha, W Premerlani, F Eddy, and W Lorenson. *Object-Oriented Modelling and Design*. Prentice Hall, 1991.

[Rei78]   R Reiter. On closed-world databases. In H Gallaire and J Minker, editors, *Logic and databases*, pages 55–76. Plenum Press, 1978.

[Rei80]   R Reiter. Default logic. *Artificial Intelligence*, 13:81–132, 1980.

[Rob77]   S Robertson. The probability ranking principle in information retrieval. *Journal of Documentation*, 33:294–304, 1977.

[RS91]   A Rappaport and R Smith. *Innovative Applications of Artificial Intelligence 2*. AAAI Press and MIT Press, 1991.

[RS94]   V. Risch and C. Schwind. Tableau-based characterization and theorem proving for default logic. *Journal of Automated Reasoning*, 13:223–242, 1994.

[Rya92]   M Ryan. Representing defaults as sentences with reduced priority. In B Nebel and W Swartout, editors, *Principles of Knowledge Representation and Reasoning: Proceedings of the Third International Conference*. Morgan Kaufmann, 1992.

[Saf87]   A Saffiotti. The artificial intelligence view of the treatment of uncertain knowledge. *Knowledge Engineering Review*, 2:75–97, 1987.

[Sal89]   G Salton. *Automatic Text Processing*. Addison-Wesley, 1989.

[SB91]   S Srinivas and J Breese. Ideal: A software package for analysis of influence diagrams. In P Bonissone, M Henrion, L Kanal, and J Lemmer, editors, *Uncertainty in Artificial Intelligence 6*. Elsevier, 1991.

[Sch86]   R Schacter. Evaluating influence diagrams. *Operations Research*, 33:871–882, 1986.

[Sch95]   T Schaub. A new methodology for query-answering in default logics via structure-oriented theorem proving. *Journal of Automated Reasoning*, 15:95–165, 1995.

[SDLC93]   D Spiegelhalter, A Dawid, S Lauritzen, and R Cowell. Bayesian analysis in expert systems. *Statistical Sciences*, 8:219–283, 1993.

[SFB90]   D Spiegelhalter, R Franklin, and K Bull. Probabilities for a medical expert system. In M Henrion, R Shachter, L Kanal, and J Lemmer, editors, *Uncertainty in Artificial Intelligence 5*, pages 285–294. Elsevier, 1990.

[SGG93]   E Sucar, D F Gillies, and D A Gillies. Objective probabilities in expert systems. *Artificial Intelligence*, 61:187–208, 1993.

[Sha76]   G Shafer. *A Mathematical Theory of Evidence*. Princeton University Press, 1976.

[Sho76]   E Shortliffe. *Computer-based Medical Consultations: MYCIN*. Elsevier, 1976.

[Sho88]   Y Shoham. *Reasoning about Change*. MIT Press, 1988.

[SK88]   R W Schwanke and G E Kaiser. Living with inconsistency in large systems. In *Proceedings of the International Workshop on Software Version and Configuration Control*, pages 98–118. B G Teubner, 1988.

[SK94]   Ph Smets and R Kennes. The transferable belief model. *Artificial Intelligence*, 66:191–234, 1994.

[SL90]   A Sheth and J Larson. Federated database systems for managing distributed, heterogeneous, and autonomous datbases. *ACM Computing Surveys*, 22:183–236, 1990.

[Sme95]   Ph Smets. Imperfect information: Imprecision and uncertainty. In Ph Smets and A Motro, editors, *Uncertainty Management in Information Systems*. Kluwer, 1995.

[SP90]   G Shafer and J Pearl, editors. *Readings in Uncertainty Reasoning*. Morgan Kaufmann, 1990.

[Spi86a]   D Spiegelhalter. Probabilistic reasoning in predictive expert systems. In L Kanal and J Lemmer, editors, *Uncertainty in Artificial Intelligence*, pages 47–68. Elsevier, 1986.

[Spi86b]   D Spiegelhalter. A statistical view of uncertainty in expert systems. In W Gale, editor, *Artificial Intelligence and Statistics*. Addison-Wesley, 1986.

[SRA90]   S Srinivas, S Russell, and A Agogino. Dynamic construction of belief networks. In M Henrion, R Shachter, L Kanal, and J Lemmer, editors, *Uncertainty in Artificial Intelligence 5*, pages 295–308. Elsevier, 1990.

[SWA+94]   G Schreiber, B Wielinga, H Akkermans, W van de Velde, and A Anjewlerden. CML: The common KADS conceptual modelling language. In L Steels, G Scheiber, and W van de Velde, editors, *A Future for Knowledge Acquisition*, volume 867 of *Lecture Notes in Artificial Intelligence*. Springer, 1994.

[TC91]   H Turtle and W B Croft. Evaluation of an inference network-based retrieval model. *ACM Transactions on information systems*, 9:187–222, 1991.

[TC92]   H Turtle and W B Croft. A comparison of text retrieval models. *The Computer Journal*, 35:279–290, 1992.

[TC95]   H Turtle and W B Croft. Uncertainty in information retrieval. In Ph Smets and A Motro, editors, *Uncertainty Management in Information Systems: From Needs to Solutions*. Kluwer, 1995.

[TK74]   A Tversky and D Kahneman. Judgement under uncertainty: Heuristics and biases. *Science*, 185:1124–1131, 1974.

[TSMD93]   R Tong, D Shapiro, B McCune, and J Dean. A rule-based approach to information retrieval: Some results and comments. In *Proceedings of the Eleventh National Conference on Artificial Intelligence*, pages 411–415, 1993.

[UHT94]   M Umano, I Hatona, and H Tamura. Fuzzy expert system shells. In *IEEE International Conference on Tools with Artificial Intelligence*, pages 219–225. IEEE Computer Society Press, 1994.

[Ull88]   J Ullman. *Principles of Database and Knowledge-base Systems*. Computer Science Press, 1988.

[Uni96]   *Data Mining*. Unicom, 1996.

[Voo93]   E Voorchees. Using wordnet to disambiguate word senses for text retrieval. In *Proceedings of the 16th ACM SIGIR Conference on Research and Development in Information Retrieval (SIGIR'93)*, pages 171–180. ACM Press, 1993.

[vR79]   C van Rijsbergen. *Information Retrieval*. Cambridge University Press, 1979.

[vR86]   C van Rijsbergen. A non-classical logic for information retrieval. *The Computer Journal*, 29:481–485, 1986.

[VV93]   B Vickery and A Vickery. Online search interface design. *The Journal of Documentation*, 49:103–187, 1993.

[WD91]   E Wendlandt and J Driscoll. Incorporating a semantic analysis into a document retrieval strategy. In A Bookstein, Y Chiaramella, G Salton, and V Raghavan, editors, *Proceedings of the 14th ACM SIGIR Conference on Research and Development in Information Retrieval (SIGIR'91)*, pages 270–278. ACM Press, 1991.

[Wel88]   M Wellman. Qualitative probabilistic networks for planning under uncertainty. In J Lemmer and L Kanal, editors, *Uncertainty in artificial intelligence 2*. Elsevier, 1988.

183

[Zad65]   L Zadeh. Fuzzy sets. *Information and control*, 8:338–353, 1965.

[Zad75]   L Zadeh. Fuzzy logic and approximate reasoning. *Synthese*, 30:407–428, 1975.

[Zad79]   L Zadeh. A theory of approximate reasoning. In J Hayes, D Michie, and L Mikulich, editors, *Machine Intelligence 9*, pages 149–194. Ellis Horwood, 1979.

[Zad83]   L Zadeh. The role of fuzzy logic in the management of uncertainty in expert systems. *Fuzzy Sets and Systems*, 11:199–227, 1983.

[Zad86]   L Zadeh. Is probability theory sufficient for dealing with uncertainty in artificial intelligence? In L Kanal and J Lemmer, editors, *Uncertainty in Artificial Intelligence*, 1986.

[Zad94]   L Zadeh. Fuzzy logic, neural networks and soft computing. *Communications of the ACM*, 37(3):77–84, 1994.

[Zic95]   R Zicari. Databases and incomplete information. In Ph Smets and A Motro, editors, *Uncertainty Management in Information Systems: From Needs to Solutions*. Kluwer, 1995.

[ZP95]   E Zimanyi and A Pirotte. Imperfect knowledge in databases. In Ph Smets and A Motro, editors, *Uncertainty Management in Information Systems: From Needs to Solutions*. Kluwer, 1995.

Index